692

$1.99

8/22/2017

CRYSTAL LAKE

Jim COURT

KNOW YOURSELF, FORGET YOURSELF

MARC LESSER

KNOW
YOURSELF,
FORGET
YOURSELF

Five Truths to Transform Your Work,
Relationships, and Everyday Life

MJF BOOKS

New York

Published by MJF Books
Fine Communications
322 Eighth Avenue
New York, NY 10001

Know Yourself, Forget Yourself
LC Control Number: 2014952668
ISBN 978-1-60671-277-1

CONTENTS

KNOW
YOURSELF,
FORGET
YOURSELF

THE THREE BRICKLAYERS

There is a story of three bricklayers working side by side that is sometimes told to illustrate the power of purpose and vision.

Someone comes along and asks the first bricklayer, "What are you doing?" The first bricklayer replies, "I'm laying bricks, one by one. Applying mortar and placing each brick."

The second bricklayer is asked, "What are you doing?" He answers, "I'm making a living. By doing this job, I'm able to provide for my family."

The third bricklayer, when asked, "What are you doing?" responds, "I'm building a cathedral. I'm helping people to connect with God."

I've always liked this story. On one level, it's a beautiful, simple illustration about perspective. It demonstrates the power we each have to choose how to interpret the events of our lives, how we can create our own unique meaning. The three bricklayers are performing the same task while understanding what they are accomplishing in completely different terms.

Looking at this story a bit more carefully, however, I wonder: if I were overseeing this project, I might be a little alarmed by the second and third answers. After all, I've hired people to lay bricks, and I might not be pleased if, while doing this task, they are distracted by thoughts of their family. I might be even more concerned if they are dreaming about some higher purpose. As a supervisor, I want my bricklayers paying attention to the details of laying bricks. Is the mortar mix the perfect proportion of sand, stone, and water? Is each person diligently looking at the blueprints and placing each brick in exactly the right place? Is each person and the team working cooperatively and yet fast enough to meet the schedule? In other words, at any one time, there are lots of tasks we could be focused on, but are we focused on the right ones? How do we know which are the right ones?

At the same time, as the supervisor, I understand that my employees are human beings, not machines. Humans have needs, emotions, aspirations. I recognize that for people to be most effective — to be able to work with skill, creativity, and conscientiousness — they need to be compensated fairly and adequately, in ways that meet their personal and family needs. And in order to be inspired to be truly excellent bricklayers, they need to be included in the work's larger vision and purpose. They must be encouraged to see the noble aspect of the work they are performing — in this case, the sacred act of building a cathedral, a spiritual gathering place for the benefit of our community. Though it feels somewhat daunting, part of my job is to help them connect the simple act of laying bricks with the divine. Embracing all these perspectives or attitudes helps us achieve the great results we seek. Ultimately, I don't want each bricklayer focused on only one aspect of their job; I want them to be adept enough to focus on, and succeed at, all three aspects simultaneously.

We are all like these three bricklayers, who together represent our individual self. The message of the story is that we each hold these differing, even contradictory perspectives within us all the time, and our continual, paradoxical task is to discover, in each moment, how to embrace, penetrate, and reconcile them effectively, cooperatively, even joyfully.

Step back and look at your daily life. Each day is filled with small tasks and activities, stuff to get done, bricks to lay. In and around these tasks, we eat, sleep, exercise, pay bills, go shopping, get the kids to and from school, and express our love. We maintain our home and family life. And during all this, we aspire and dream and connect with others. We are always aware, in some part of ourselves, of our aspiration toward our life's greater goals. We are often assessing whether our work and activity is meaningful, if it has a larger purpose and benefits others. Like the three bricklayers, we are balancing multiple states of awareness even as we attend to the details of the specific job at hand, trying to do good work, take care of our family life, and find connection and fulfillment.

I enjoy using parables, and the bricklayer story arose recently during a meeting with one of my executive coaching clients, Roger, who is the CEO of an insurance company. Roger was describing how he was feeling increasingly tired and stressed from the day-to-day activities of his business — negotiating contracts, managing employees, and developing new business. At times he spoke about his work with great enthusiasm. He understood that from a larger perspective he was in the business of helping people create more security for themselves and their families. But as a source of greater meaning and inspiration, this wasn't enough. His enthusiasm was flagging, and with it his effectiveness in his job. We discussed the three bricklayers story and the contradictions and tensions of integrating our daily work with vision, purpose, and our sense of community and well-being.

I was surprised to see tears in Roger's eyes as he entered more deeply into the ways these issues impacted his life. We began to address how he might transform the stress he felt into more equanimity and enthusiasm, how he might improve his ability to focus and develop the quality of his attention. At the end of his workday he wanted to be less distracted and tense and more present and alive for his family. At the same time, he wanted to better understand how to shift the culture of his organization from one that was often cynical to one that encouraged trust, collaboration, and innovation. He wondered how he and the people he worked with could develop more responsiveness and compassion while simultaneously improving the effectiveness and profitability of the business.

This is the same challenge and opportunity many of us face every day: How can we be present and alive for each moment of our lives in ways that allow us to actually *feel* alive in every moment? I believe it is only by embracing our life's contradictions that we understand how to work with them and find clarity, balance, and meaning within the context of our particular circumstances. On the surface, this counterintuitive approach itself seems contradictory. But in my life and in my work, I have found that embracing life's paradoxes is a powerful skill; it is a path to increasing effectiveness, awakening joy, and discovering our true purpose, in this and each new moment. Our minds are the most engaged and vibrant when we honor complexity, learn stillness in turmoil, face doubt with confidence, and seek to know ourselves so that we might better serve others.

There is no laminated foldout map for becoming more balanced and alive. There is no single established path, though conventional wisdom often promises that such a path exists. Indeed, one of our biggest obstacles is the doubt and anxiety we feel about whether we are on the right path, about whether we are acting effectively, helpfully, and appropriately. However, there are reliable, effective methods for creating the path we need, one fitted to ourselves, and that is what this book offers. It's a program for finding our way whenever we feel lost, and in part it uses contradictions and paradoxes like signposts that can help point us in a clearer direction. Humans are inescapable storytellers, and we can hold many stories at the same time. The elasticity of the human mind not only is capable of this but seems to welcome the chance. This book seeks to help you name and embrace your life's contradictory truths, its authentic paradoxes, as essential to creating an inspired, effective life.

To do this, I use and have developed a number of surprisingly simple tools and practices, which are designed to be easy to remember and integrate into your daily life. Simplicity is good, because navigating our relationships, our work life, and our place in the larger world can be difficult, confusing, and complex. That is why I find stories and parables like that of the three bricklayers so useful. In their paradoxical ways, they wake us up to what is obvious and true, and they can help us recognize what we don't otherwise see.

Over many years, working with my clients and in my own life, I've distilled these paradoxes into five core truths. Each represents an important understanding, a vital competency, and a way of living in the world that leads to greater freedom, satisfaction, and effectiveness. They are

1. Know yourself, forget yourself
2. Be confident, question everything
3. Fight for change, accept what is
4. Embrace emotion, embody equanimity
5. Benefit others, benefit yourself

Each of these five truths is a paradox — a paradox that can be embraced and practiced. Together these five truths can be worked with as a program or a path.

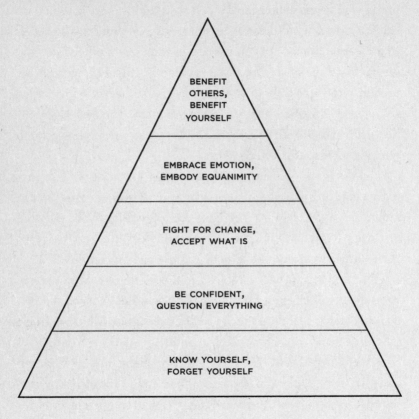

Another way to work with these paradoxical truths is to identify the results of practicing each truth, and to recognize that each truth builds upon the preceding truth:

- By working with "know yourself, forget yourself," you develop your *attention*.
- By working with "be confident, question everything," you broaden your *outlook*.

- By working with "fight for change, accept what is," you foster more skillful *action*.
- By working with "embrace emotion, embody equanimity," you increase your *resilience*.
- By working with "benefit others, benefit yourself," you gain *effectiveness*.

The program or path of working with each of these paradoxical truths leads, progressively, to developing your attention, outlook, action, resilience, and effectiveness:

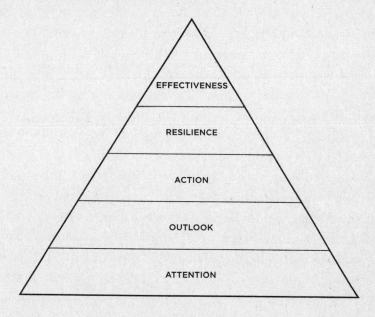

This book is organized in two parts. In part 1, I explain the book's central concepts and methods. Chapter 1 discusses what I mean by "paradox" and how embracing it leads to greater clarity and insight. I also introduce myself and explain how I grew into a paradoxical combination of Zen teacher, CEO, and leadership consultant. Chapter 2 explains what I mean by "effectiveness,"

and it describes the book's practical approach and how to use the book to create your own path. Chapter 3 discusses the Zen Buddhist concepts that underlie much of the material, and it explains how to read and work with the teaching stories that I use throughout.

Then part 2 presents the five core truths. These are five essential areas where we primarily seek and most need effectiveness. Knowing, in any particular situation, what an appropriate response should be almost always involves embracing the knotty riddles and contradictions in one or more of these five arenas. In all cases, by seeing the ways we are out of balance in these areas, we can learn what we need to do to recover our balance and become more effective. Throughout, I use real-world stories from my clients' lives and my own life to show how this works.

In Buddhism, the path to awakening is often called "the middle way." It is the path we tread between the extremes and opposing forces of life. However, I've found that this terminology can be misleading. It suggests something akin to "moderation in all things," as if we might resolve these contradictions into a single perfect, correct action that strikes a middle ground. But that is not how we experience life, nor is it a recipe for fulfillment and success. For instance, there are times when we must act with bold assurance, and times when we must patiently refrain from acting or even voicing our opinion at all. In either case, half measures will not do. Instead, we have to train ourselves to be able to act in whatever way is most skillful at any one time, choosing from among all possibilities. We must hold the contradictions and paradoxes within us, balancing them in a continual dance that enriches, enlivens, and often unexpectedly relaxes our lives in the process.

As the book's title suggests, the imperative to know yourself and forget yourself represents perhaps the central paradox that we must face. All the other paradoxes relate to it in some way. In addition, throughout history, many other schools of thought have espoused this conundrum, that we are to deeply know ourselves while at the same time managing to be selfless. "Know thyself" was, famously, the inscription on the Temple of Apollo at Delphi in ancient Greece. Ralph Waldo Emerson preached that knowing yourself was essential for finding God within, although Christianity has often said the opposite, that forgetting yourself is the path to God. Eihei Dogen, the founder of Zen Buddhism in thirteenth-century Japan, said, "To study the Way is to study the self. To study the self is to forget the self." Yet however one frames this apparent riddle, the goal has always been to understand and deeply experience the profound mystery of consciousness, of our place within the sacred, while simultaneously finding fulfillment, effectiveness, and compassion in daily life.

The stakes for doing this are high, and the benefits of success are pragmatic and urgently needed. Our world is messy and difficult. The list of human-made problems is daunting: climate change, war, violence, severe economic injustice, underemployment. Writer, businessman, and environmental visionary Paul Hawken once said that "humans are the only species on the planet with an unemployment problem. Brilliant!" On this score, the Buddhists got it right — underlying all these seemingly unsolvable problems are the same basic human tendencies: greed, hate, and delusion. Isn't this the level in which the real problems of our world exist? Imagine if we focused here. Imagine if we used this as our inspiration: to heal ourselves, and in this way also, in a real and direct manner, heal the world.

This is my highest and truest hope for the work that I do and for this book. I often end my workshops and retreats by saying that my real hope is to create a conspiracy. The word *conspiracy* literally means "breathing together": *con* means "with"; *spire* is "to breathe." Together, we can change the world, beginning with ourselves. We do this by combining and integrating these attention and mindfulness practices, the skills of influence, leadership, and real power, along with ethical, responsible, and compassionate actions. When we are successful, we can bring skillful action, compassion, and wisdom into our daily lives and activities. We can change the world through our own sense of presence, our ability to show up, to be ourselves, to speak the truth.

When my daughter was seven years old I used to read to her every night before she went to sleep. One night as we were completing our nightly routine, she turned to me and said, "Daddy, when we die, do you think we are given all the answers about life — like when you play a board game and you are done, and you look at the back for the solutions?"

The truth is I don't remember exactly what I said. I hope I said something like "I don't think we need to wait until we are dying to find the answers. I think that real wisdom, real compassion, and real love are right here, right now, in every moment."

When we pay attention, right in the midst of the difficulties and strains, the pleasures and pains of our lives, it's the unexpected, the puzzles, the paradoxes that catch us, open us, change us. We can appreciate and learn from these puzzles, and little by little, or all at once, solutions appear. We have the ability to transform and shape the context of our lives and become skillful, excellent bricklayers: doing our work well, taking good care of ourselves and our families, and taking care of others and the world.

Breathing, together.

Part 1

EMBRACE PARADOX

Chapter 1

FROM PARADOX TO INSIGHT

Can't say what I'm doing here,
But I hope to see much clearer
After living in the material world.

— GEORGE HARRISON, "LIVING IN THE MATERIAL WORLD"

I was recently sitting in the office of a senior executive of a major corporation in the San Francisco Bay Area. We were meeting for the first time. His manager had told me that he was a high-performing leader who was now underperforming. During our conversation the executive shared with me his disappointment about work. "What happened?" he pondered. He had begun this job with such excitement and enthusiasm, such belief in his ability to do a great job and achieve lofty goals. Now he felt discouraged and exhausted. Then he shared with me that he had a similar feeling in his marriage and family life.

He said, "How did I get so busy and yet manage to feel so uninspired? Why does my life feel stale? Why do I have a gnawing sense of defeat much of the time? To the world I seem dynamic and productive, but internally I am either churning or numb. What happened to the enthusiasm and excitement I had for life when I was young, just setting out in my career and marriage? When did my life get so out of balance?"

His eyes looked pained, and his shoulders were slightly hunched. Behind him, I noticed a nearly life-size wooden cutout

of a rhinoceros. How odd, I thought. What was this large crea-
ture doing lurking in the office of this senior executive? "What is
that?" I asked.

The man smiled for the first time during our meeting. "Oh,
that was from an event that we held about fifteen years ago. Since
there was no place to store it and I didn't want it thrown out, this
rhino has been living in my office ever since."

"That image reminds me of a story," I told him. "It's an old
Zen story that goes like this: A teacher says to his attendant, 'Bring
me my fan, the rhinoceros horn fan.' Apparently, the teacher had
a special fan that either had a painting of a rhinoceros or perhaps
was made with some sliver of rhinoceros horn. The attendant
responds, 'I'm afraid your rhinoceros horn fan is broken.' "

I stopped and asked the executive, "What do you think the
teacher said?"

The man shrugged. He didn't know.

I told him, "The teacher stated sternly, 'Then bring me the
rhinoceros!' "

We both chuckled. It's a silly, preposterous story that makes
about as much apparent sense as the rhinoceros in this executive's
office.

I asked the executive to look at his rhinoceros. I asked him
to remember what he felt like, bringing it into his office many
years ago. It must have been lighthearted, risky, surprising. "Yes,"
he acknowledged and smiled. "I was new to my job, excited and
nervous."

"Let's see if we can bring back some of that surprise, that
energy, into your work and life right now," I responded. "Some
of that rhinoceros energy!"

The Zen story is about surprise and creative energy. The
teacher is saying to his attendant, Wake up! Don't take your life

for granted. Don't take anything for granted. Think, consider, and live outside of your habitual ways. I explained this to the executive and told him, "Your whole life is right here, right now! So let's begin by having you pay attention to the simple and obvious parts of your life that you may be overlooking. Let's talk about what is working that brings you joy as well as what you avoid, what annoys and angers you. Just as the teacher used what was directly in front of him, let's work with what is right in front of you."

In my role as an executive coach, I help people become more effective, to lead a more effective life. I help them see how they contribute to their own lack of effectiveness and then help them develop the skills and strategies to remove these obstacles. This may sound simple, but nothing is simple when you are growing and developing as a leader and as a person, moving beyond the assumptions and habits that were previously successful but are no longer adequate, or when you are stuck, unsure what to do, at a dead end, or despairing. My role is to unlock what resides within leaders and/or to help them develop new ways of seeing or new competencies. I often describe my work as helping clients to see openings and possibilities that they may not be aware of. At times these openings appear obvious. Other times they are more subtle. Then, once these openings are named, I help people to step forward, exploring and saying yes to this potential.

Clients come to me because they, or the people around them, are experiencing what I call creative gaps — gaps between where people are and where they need or want to be. In other words, they have an opportunity for growth. At times, this gap is experienced as painful; sometimes there's an emotional breakdown or some troubling or disabling imbalance in their life. Typically, the difficulty is presented as work related — the people are in transition and need to increase leadership skills, team-building skills, or communication skills. Or they know (or have been told by a mentor, colleague, supervisor, boss, or their board) that they have an opportunity for improvement in their job, or they are struggling, or both. They acknowledge that they can, and need to be, more effective in their current position.

My role as an effectiveness coach is to shift their immediate work issues, but paradoxically, to do this I must address, and shift, the person's entire way of looking at themselves and the world. Simply put, my goal is to help them wake up — to their work, to themselves, to appreciation and curiosity; to life itself.

The Usefulness of Paradox

To thrive in our lives, and be happy and effective, we must be in balance; on a very real level, our personal life, work life, and spiritual life are not at all separate. But how do we achieve balance? More importantly, how do we keep our balance when life seems designed to knock us off balance? One answer is to become as adept as a tightrope walker. A tightrope walker can feel when he or she slips out of balance and adjust, stepping more quickly or not at all, bending a little to the left, now to the right. As an audience, we see the acrobat losing balance and know that the person will fall if it goes uncorrected. Indeed, that's the entertainment. We marvel at how the tightrope walker shifts in and out of balance constantly and continually, moving back and forth across the wire while performing tricks that only increase the difficulty. How, we wonder, does the person do it?

Acrobats achieve this skill through practice, by understanding and honing their kinetic sense of inner balance. They come to know their internal gyroscope so well that they can feel every wobble and instinctively correct it. They also learn to balance their inner and outer awareness while never losing focus on the present moment: as performers, they must remember their audience and the show itself even as they adjust for every shift in their environment and in their physical position on the wire. They need to be absolutely in-the-moment about themselves and also hold in mind the next trick, the show's progress.

This isn't easy. In order to find balance you must be open and responsive to imbalance. This is the paradox of the tightrope walker.

I have come to believe that embracing and responding to paradox — turning our assumptions upside down, expecting the unexpected, comfortably holding two opposing viewpoints at the same time, resolving conflicting requirements, and so on — is the key to waking up to ourselves and the present moment and discovering the right thing to do. Paradox is the doorway to insight, just as falling is necessary for learning how to balance on a tightrope. We all want more clarity, more ease, more connectedness, more possibilities, more compassion, more kindness. We want healthy relationships in order to thrive at our work and to be effective in all areas of our life. What is hard is knowing in any given situation what the appropriate action or response should be. We want the insight to know how to achieve all these things, but our vision and experience are limited.

There is an expression from the Zen tradition, "Don't be a board-carrying fellow." This refers to the image of a carpenter carrying a wide wooden board on his or her shoulder. The board blocks and limits vision, allowing the carpenter to see only one side of things. This expression is meant to caution us from thinking we see fully and clearly, when we see only partially. We are all board-carrying fellows. We usually just see the world from our ordinary, habitual viewpoint and neglect the mysterious, the profound, the obvious. If we don't know or acknowledge that our viewpoint is limited, we will find it virtually impossible to gain the insight that allows us to respond in new, more successful ways. To become aware of our limitations, to achieve the insights we crave, we need to wake up.

Accepting the power of paradox is one of life's ways of waking us up, shocking us into awareness, so we can find our balance again. Waking up can be cultivated, practiced, so that it becomes a way of life, so that it becomes our habitual approach to life. Then we may become as skillful as a tightrope walker, who lives on the edge of falling and yet (almost) always catches him- or herself in time.

Paradox means many things and can be worked with and utilized in our lives in many ways. Many Zen stories embody or are steeped in paradox, and I use them often in my work, as I do in this book. Yet paradox can also simply be a startling, peculiar, playful, or unexpected observation that challenges our habitual way of thinking. It is asking, "What is this rhinoceros doing in my office?" It is the late anthropologist Gregory Bateson observing that spaceship Earth is so well designed that we have no idea we are on one. Here we are, hurtling through space at a million miles per hour with no need for seat belts, plenty of room in coach, and excellent food. Imagine. Paradox is anytime you hear that whisper in your ear, "Wake up, the world is extraordinary. This life you take for granted isn't what you think!"

The Five Truths

Shunryu Suzuki, the founder of the San Francisco Zen Center, once proclaimed in a public talk, "The secret of Zen is just two words... *not always so*." He and the audience laughed. He clarified that in Japanese, his native language, this expression can be stated in two words. How funny and appropriate that the statement itself exemplified his point. Whatever we think, life is not so simple... and yet it is.

Speaking personally, I'm not happy or satisfied with the idea of paradox. I don't really want this book to be about paradox; I want this book to be about clarity. Who wants paradoxical relationships, or paradox in business? We all want confidence and assurance. Imagine a stockbroker or surgeon or soldier using the word *paradox* to describe his or her work. Paradox seems the opposite of clarity, the opposite of action, a nonanswer; for some, a shrug.

In my work life and personal life, I've come to realize that embracing what is obvious is not always so easy. Meanwhile, paradox can point to a radical clarity. My hope is that this book will help you see that with paradox comes a kind of clarity that is more accurate, more true, more clear than clear, than what we usually accept at face value. Life and death *are* a paradox; in our day-to-day lives, we are constantly torn between opposites and dualities, between competing desires and needs. There is no escaping the paradoxical nature of the world. If we accept this, and meet paradox head on, if we work with and penetrate these apparently unsolvable conundrums, the place we reach is insight.

This insight can express itself uniquely in any situation and yet embody universal truths. I have found it useful to distill this work into five core insights. These five insights present themselves as paradoxes, or seemingly conflicting statements, but nevertheless, they hold the keys to right action, effectiveness, and balance.

The five truths we will explore in this book are

• The skill, in every moment, to know ourselves fully and forget ourselves entirely

- The trust to be confident in the face of doubt and to have the confidence to question everything
- The discernment to know when to act to improve our lives and the world and when to accept life as it is, as events present themselves
- The openness and capacity to embrace our emotions, our joys and pains, and find calm and composure in the midst of the demands of work and life, in the midst of difficulty and change
- The wisdom to turn toward helping others and healing the world while simultaneously caring for and developing ourselves

These truths are meant to be practiced, not merely understood or studied. Through practice, we can learn to clarify and shift our habits so that we are more successful in our everyday lives. For instance, sometimes the way we protect ourselves brings us unnecessary pain and suffering; we react to our fear and anxiety in ways that cut off or compromise our experience of kindness and compassion. Often, I've found, the most effective solutions are counterintuitive: we must allow pain to feel less pain. We must let go of our desire in order to gain what we want. We must heal our spiritual problems to solve our work problems, or our family problems, or vice versa. We must accept that we are all things all at once in the only moment that counts, this one.

For instance, I am present, right here and now, and I am also reviewing the past and thinking about the future. I live in this moment, spacious, present, and curious. And I'm aware of this new moment, this sense of living on the edge of the wave of time. My life feels full and, when I look deeply, also empty. I laughed many times today, and I also cried, and the pain and release of tears made me feel full and happy. During the most recent winter holidays, the happiness of being with my family was wonderful and full of loss and sadness — knowing that not only would these moments not last, but that these lives would not last. I was both pained and proud to wave good-bye to my twenty-four-year-old daughter, as she drove away with a caring and sensitive young man at her side.

When someone asks about the status of my work life, I'm often tempted to answer that I'm on the verge of both tremendous success and tremendous failure. I can list all the things that are making this a good year: new skills I've learned and ways I've grown, the money I've earned, the projects I've completed, the positive impacts of my coaching and consulting work. I can also list all the errors I've made, the failed projects, the missed opportunities, and all the more and better things I have yet to achieve. Depending on my mood, I might prefer one list or the other, but both are valid and true; neither is the whole story.

We are all spiritual creatures masquerading as practical creatures. That is, when we are not practical creatures masquerading as spiritual creatures. I know that washing the dishes can be just washing the dishes. Sometimes they just need to get cleaned and put away, ready for the next meal. Washing the dishes can be incredibly tedious and boring. It can also be a sensual event, paying attention, noticing the feeling of warm water touching the hands, the hardness of the plates, the sharpness of the silverware. It can be a communal act, sharing the burden of household chores; even thinking to do them at all could be an expression of loving attention to those you live with. It can also be a spiritual act, just being present, giving yourself over to an activity with gentle enthusiasm and gratitude for your home and nourishment, or of letting go of self-concern and self-awareness. Just washing the dishes. Having no other thought or ulterior motive. Imagine, if this were the first time, your first experience in dishwashing, seeing a dish and water and hands come together. Or imagine, perhaps this will be the last time. Never again will you have this experience.

In any one moment, all of these things can exist, whether we are washing dishes, commuting to work, writing a check, giving a presentation, hiking in the woods, or making love. Typically, we choose how we want to experience something and that guides our actions. Then, when and if we experience difficulties or unhappiness, insight is whatever wakes us up so that we see the choice we've made. Insight is understanding that we have, in fact, made a choice (that we are board-carrying fellows), and thus we can choose differently and change our approach to the task or interaction. Insight is recognizing that we are imbalanced and then discerning how, specifically, we need to shift our perspective and actions to come back to balance. This is a never-ending process and challenge. Yet by following the five insight practices in this book, we can learn to walk this tightrope. We can learn to distinguish and balance our own self-interest, the interests of others, the interests of our companies and communities, and even the interests of our ecosystems and planet. This subtle, profound practice can't be made with the thinking mind alone. It involves thinking and feeling, action and acceptance, selfishness and compassion, right brain and left brain, head, heart, body, and soul.

Resolute and Clear, Unfathomable Gate

My entire adult life, I have been a Zen student and a businessman. I am a CEO, MBA, and Zen teacher. For the past eight years, I have run a consulting practice (ZBA Associates) as an executive coach for businesspeople at major corporations (such as Google,

Twitter, Genentech, and Facebook) and at nonprofit organizations throughout the United States and the world.

When I was twenty-one years old, I took a one-year leave of absence from Rutgers University in New Jersey and traveled to California. This did not please my parents, but I knew I needed a break from academics. At the time, I had no clue that this journey would turn into ten years of living at the San Francisco Zen Center, or that my Zen training would result in a new name and a calling.

During this time I lived at all three of the San Francisco Zen Center's locations — two years in San Francisco, three years at Green Gulch Farm in Marin County, and five years at Tassajara Zen Mountain Center, the first Zen monastery in the Western world. As a Zen student I practiced sitting meditation with a community of about fifty people every morning and every afternoon. I found Zen philosophy and practice to be a wise, inclusive, deeply spiritual, nonjudgmental explanation of reality. It provides ethical constructs, community guidelines, and a physical practice. My work at the center was varied and nearly always stretched my sense of myself and my capabilities — I was trained as a bread baker, cook, and draft horse farmer, and during my tenth year at the Zen Center, I was director of Tassajara.

After five years, it became time for my Buddhist Lay Ordination Ceremony. The ceremony primarily involved anchoring my life to "do good, avoid harm, and help others." In Buddhism these are called the "three pure precepts," or practices, for purifying the mind. To me, the ceremony was expressing that practicing meditation, and living a meditative life, was a central part of my life, and this was one way to publicly make this statement. Since the Zen Center is part of the Japanese Soto Zen tradition, I spent a year sewing by hand a small version of what is thought of as

Buddha's robe, a small piece of cloth about the size of a bib, that is worn around the neck. The pattern of the robe is modeled after a rice field, as in China, where these were originally developed. Each stitch is sewn by hand, and you affirm your intention to practice with each stitch. These were originally developed so that monks could wear robes while farming and doing other forms of manual labor.

As part of this ceremony, I was given a new Buddhist name, which was bestowed by the then-thirty-nine-year-old spiritual leader, or abbot, of the San Francisco Zen Center, Richard Baker. The name Richard chose for me: Benefit Decree, Material Gate.

I was completely puzzled by this name. The first part, Benefit Decree, seemed to be saying that I was being requested to make my life a way of benefiting others. This felt right, and I was both comforted and challenged by this part of my name.

Material Gate, the second part of my name, was more difficult to understand or connect with. I pictured a large opening, a gate, something that I needed to walk through, and that somehow this gate was connected to the world of work, or money, the world of material things — in contrast to the world of ideas or philosophy.

Over the next several years, I puzzled over what this bizarre name meant for me. By my tenth year, as Tassajara director, I was surprised to wake up one morning and notice that, though I was a Zen monk, I was also running a business. As Tassajara director, I was responsible for a million-dollar budget, a staff of sixty, and the problems and challenges of an organization serving seventy overnight guests daily. I was surprised how much I enjoyed leadership, and even more surprised at not only the lack of conflict between leadership and spiritual practice but by how well they integrated and informed each other. Leadership, management, and spiritual practice are all about seeing more clearly, finding creative solutions, and waking up!

This profound insight revealed the deeper meaning of my name, and I decided to devote my work life to this mission — to integrating contemplative and work practices, to changing the world by helping business leaders become more aware, awake, and wise, and doing all these things to solve real problems. This set the course for my own personal, professional, and spiritual growth: I would step into a mission that was large and audacious, I would do something very different and unexpected from the path I thought I would take, and I would take it one step at a time.

Naturally, paradoxically, my first step was to leave Tassajara and enroll at New York University's Graduate School of Business, which was on Wall Street at that time, to pursue a leadership education and MBA degree. Then, in 1989, three years after graduating from business school, I founded and was CEO of Brush Dance, a publishing company that made inspirational greeting cards and calendars from recycled paper.

Brush Dance began literally in my garage as one of the first companies in the world to make products out of recycled paper. Over the next fifteen years, Brush Dance grew and evolved into a multimillion-dollar company producing beautiful and inspirational cards, journals, and calendars that touched the lives of millions. However, like every successful CEO, I earned my stripes as much through my failures as through my successes: failed initiatives, failed products, failed hires. As the business maxim goes, I learned the most from my failures, even though failure was the last thing I wanted. Like every business owner, I felt passionately about my company, and I poured all my creativity, brainpower, pride, personal capital, and time into its success.

During the years I grew Brush Dance, I learned a huge amount about business and managing people, and even more about myself. I discovered that the energized, innovative, high-stakes business world can be immensely rewarding, even with all the financial setbacks and stress that perpetually hover around it. I learned that I have a proclivity and passion for financial fore-casting, product development, and marketing. Most important, I found that, surprisingly, I love working in the for-profit world, and I was particularly drawn to the people, the human side of business — to the importance of trust, of teamwork and col-laboration.

However, in 2004, I decided it was time to step down from Brush Dance. After fifteen years as CEO, I found my heart was no longer in the publishing business. This was disorienting and painful since I had started the company. Yet as I privately planned my transition, I was preemptively fired by my board of directors. This felt like a major failure, and in the aftermath, I was forced to honestly assess how my waning creativity and leadership helped lead to this outcome. This assessment, and these lessons, only increased my resolve to help others in business, and over the next several years, I successfully launched the executive consulting company ZBA Associates.

Through these years, I also continued to develop my Zen training, and I was ordained as a Zen priest in 2003. During my priest ordination ceremony, my teacher at the time, Norman Fischer, decided to change the first part of my name, to make it more direct; he called me Resolute and Clear, Material Gate. He thought that the second part of my name was perfect, mirroring the way in which my work life revolved around bringing spiritual practices into the business world.

Or perhaps not, for in 2011, my name was changed again. My

teacher at that time, Michael Wenger, decided the last part of my name needed fine-tuning. As I was completing the last stage of my formal Zen training (known as Dharma Transmission), he changed my name to Resolute and Clear, Unfathomable Gate. Yes, a paradox, one that Michael felt is more aligned and representative of me and my practice today. While I remain challenged by my Zen name, I am no longer confused by it. Though it was given to me, I see it as representing the human condition. We all aspire to be resolute, to have a firm conviction, and to be clear. Yet, counterintuitively and paradoxically, the path, the gate, the experience and trajectory of our lives — all of these are deep, profound, and unfathomable.

Just the other day, I co-led a "day of mindfulness" at Google's headquarters in Mountain View, California, as part of the mindfulness-based emotional intelligence program called Search Inside Yourself. The last exercise of the day was an exploration called the Game of Self. Two people sit facing each other and, in turn and repeatedly, ask each other who they are.

To demonstrate, my colleague Meng asked me, "Marc, who are you?"

I responded, "I am a Zen priest, a CEO businessman, a father, husband, son."

"Marc, who are you?" Meng asked again.

"I am compassionate, courageous, vulnerable," I replied. "I am this body and mind, and I am more than this body and mind. I am playful, searching, caring. I love to laugh and appreciate my tears. I am passionate and calm. I love to teach and to learn. I am an explorer."

We then had all forty people in the class get into pairs and play the Game of Self.

This simple game has a variety of purposes. We learn that our idea of who we are is deeper, wider, and more complex than our usual biographies or elevator speeches about ourselves. We are so many things! And we can see that, though all of these statements may be true, none of these descriptions or labels defines us. What we each often think of as "me" is extremely limited and may in fact not even exist.

In my work now, I help clients create a more interconnected view of their work-related life and their emotional landscape, the latter being the part of their life that is sometimes the greatest and most mysterious part of who they are. I then try to help them brighten and further balance these two elements with something I believe is essential to the deepest human happiness: spiritual fulfillment. It is the sense of the sacred (not necessarily religious) that fills us with a profound sense of wonder and awe and that uplifts us.

When these dimensions are integrated, we are able to accomplish more, with fewer distractions. We can do more of what we wish to do, with less stress. This was the theme of my previous book, *Less*, which made this promise in four words: Accomplish more. Do less. Yes, a paradox! This book builds on the premise of *Less* while focusing on *surprise* — on how we can utilize surprising statements and surprising practices to enliven, wake up, and transform our personal, professional, and spiritual life.

I believe we are all Zen students and all businesspeople. Zen is the practice of being a vibrant, effective human being while embracing our pains and vulnerabilities as an essential part of being fully alive. Zen is the practice of finding our innate freedom and practicing compassion in the midst of the stark reality that we are born and we will die. Zen is responding to the needs, problems, and cries of the world with effectiveness and with an open heart. And we are all businesspeople, whether teachers or doctors or nonprofit executives or homemakers or salespeople working the aisles of Walmart. There is no avoiding the need for money, goods, and services. No avoiding the material world. My passion in life is to help people to become more present, alive, and awake, to help people integrate — balance — their work life, spiritual life, and personal life, and to do so in the very real material world.

Chapter 2

EFFECTIVENESS: THE BACKWARD STEP

So teach us to number our days
that we may attain a heart of wisdom.

— PSALM 90:12

As an executive coach, I recently began working with Gail, who is an executive director of a large and complex non-profit organization. She is thirty-four years old, much younger than the woman who previously held this leadership position. Gail was thrilled, surprised, and nervous to find herself in a role with so much authority and responsibility. As she was describing her work and personal challenges to me, I looked at her and said, "Do you realize that you hold your breath while you are speaking? It is subtle, but I wonder what your experience is?" Tears welled in her eyes. She described how, when speaking, she felt underlying fear and anxiety most of the time. She was aware that she tended to edit her words before she spoke, and she was also aware of a general lack of trust in herself.

Right then, we began to practice breathing together, counting 1, 2, 3, 4, 5 on the out-breath, and 1, 2, 3 on the in-breath. I asked her to explore a feeling of confidence with each exhale, followed by a sense of curiosity on the inhale. Confidently and completely breathing out. Waiting to see what will happen next. Exploring the experience of not knowing and not controlling. Discovering how the inhale happens without any effort. In the moment,

Gail's anxiety lessened noticeably, and I instructed her to continue this practice every day, as well as whenever she noticed she had stopped breathing. The practice I suggested she explore, during the next seven days, was to begin noticing whenever she was holding herself back, to just notice what was happening, with her thinking, with her body, with her breath.

This led to a discussion of the way in which she experienced her work and life as having one foot on the gas and the other foot on the brake. Whenever she would feel confidence (foot on the gas), she would then be filled with anxiety, self-doubt, and the fear of making a mistake or being misunderstood (foot on the brake). She would have good ideas but then hold back. This limited her ability to be completely present and to communicate clearly, and this ultimately limited her effectiveness. I pointed out that this caution, this tightening, limited her chances of failing but also of experiencing success and joy.

What was so touching in our interchange is that she realized that something as simple as breathing more fully as she spoke greatly enhanced her presence; it improved her own sense of power and effectiveness in her work and relationships. We talked about the importance of feeling comfortable and being confident when you don't know what will happen. In this case, balance and effectiveness don't mean finding a middle ground. They mean: When you are confident, be fully confident. When you are saying no or feeling cautious, say no or be fully cautious. When it is time to go or to act, don't put your foot on the brake, and when it's time to stop, don't keep pressing the gas pedal.

This insight about balance and effectiveness opened up realms of new possibilities for Gail. She found the courage and the skills she needed to have some difficult conversations with her boss regarding how her boss's rough and judgmental communication style was negatively impacting the organization's effectiveness. Her personal life began to shift as she expressed herself more openly and clearly to her partner. And her relationship with her parents, which had always been strained, transformed as she began to be much more confident in herself and more curious and interested in her parents' perspective and experience. As we worked together over several months, Gail became a much more responsive and effective leader and person.

What Is Effectiveness?

Not long ago, I was in Berkeley for a coaching meeting with Kaz Tanahashi, one of my clients. I don't usually mention my clients by name, but at social events, Kaz introduces me as his coach, and he gave me permission to use his name here. Kaz is a world-renowned calligrapher, writer, and translator. He has written or translated more than a dozen books and is currently in the midst of several book projects. At age seventy-nine he travels around the world speaking on environmentalism and peace and teaching calligraphy and Zen. When I mentioned to him that I was in the middle of writing a book focused on effectiveness, he looked at me and asked, "Are *you* effective?"

For a second I was taken aback, but of course, what a great question! It asks not only whether I am offering a useful, practical definition of effectiveness, but also if I am myself effective in my own life? Will I be an effective teacher of effectiveness.

Like most people, sometimes I feel extremely effective, and yet more often I feel I could or should be even more effective. Sometimes I feel effective in just one or two parts of my life — perhaps my work is progressing nicely — while other parts of my life may feel stale or lacking. In time, inevitably, my sense of my own effectiveness will shift, and what once worked may no longer be successful, and places where I've been frustrated or challenged may resolve into wonderful blessings and joy. Each situation, relationship, and day is different.

There is a Zen story from the seventh century in China, part of a collection that has been passed down through the centuries. In the story, a student approaches his old and sick teacher, who is near the end of his days. The student asks, "What is the teaching of an entire lifetime?" Sometimes this question is translated as, "What is the teaching of a thousand lifetimes?"

The teacher answers, "An appropriate response."

An appropriate response — knowing when to speak or to be silent, to say yes or to say no, to stay or to leave. Knowing when to pick it up and when to put it down, when to move toward a person or situation and when to walk away. Knowing the right thing to do in any given situation — this is the definition, the key, to effectiveness. My former publishing company, Brush Dance, once published a greeting card that said, "Wisdom is knowing what to do next." Management guru Peter Drucker defined effectiveness in very similar terms: *getting the right things done.*

How do you respond in a quiet, intimate moment and in the midst of chaos? How do you respond to a child crying in the street and to the cries of the world? How do you show up and act, or react, in each situation? This is the work of a lifetime. An appropriate response means to express yourself in a way that is completely in tune with yourself, with the particular situation, and with life. An appropriate response is not a moral judgment. What we do may include a sense of what's right and wrong, good and bad, but it is a much wider, deeper, and more inclusive understanding than the quick and partial judgments to which our minds often cling.

In Chinese, the word *appropriate* contains three characters, which can be translated as "meet," "each," and "teach." This implies that our task is to respond in a way that meets each situation, each person, each of our own emotions. By doing this, there is some teaching, some learning, some wisdom that happens. The Chinese character *ichi*, translated as "each," can also mean "oneness." This points toward a further understanding: sometimes we are learning, sometimes we are teaching, and most of the time we are both learning and teaching. It also implies a level of inclusiveness. Zen sometimes describes this inclusiveness, this oneness, as "not one, not two."

My friend Pamela Weiss, who named her leadership consulting company An Appropriate Response, tells the story of a time she heard a student ask the Zen teacher Kobun Chino about his work with the dying. A young woman said to Kobun, "I've heard you often go to the bedsides of dying people. When you go to visit, how do you help them?" Hearing this question, he closed his eyes, tilted his head, and responded, "Help them? I don't help them. I meet them." Then he paused several long minutes, looked at the woman, and said, "I think, really, they help me."

Three Circles, One Insight

Then again, there's the challenge. How do we know what an appropriate action is? Defining effectiveness is much easier than knowing how to be effective in any particular moment. This entire book is devoted to helping you identify and practice right action. However, we can start by heeding the advice of the Zen teacher Dogen, who instructs his students to "take the backward step."

Backward, as Dogen uses it, means many things, but he uses it first of all as a paradoxical way to wake us up, to shake us out of the habit of blindly pushing forward (or blindly running away) whenever we encounter difficulties. Instead, in order to move forward, step back. Look, see, explore, understand. Notice confusion itself and step back in order to see it better. Step back, even, from all your ideas of who you think you are.

How? As was the case for Gail, this may mean remembering to breathe or regaining your inner composure and awareness. In general, practicing and increasing inner awareness is how we become more fully ourselves, more fully authentic human beings. Stepping backward in this way allows us to embrace and revive our natural wisdom and freedom, our True Nature (as it is often referred to in the Zen tradition).

From this place, we can begin to solve our problems. We can identify the limits of our knowledge and the impacts of our choices. This is where the dualities and oppositions of paradox are helpful, for they provide a useful framework for understanding the full and complex nature of our problems, and thus for finding solutions. Part 2 looks at these paradoxes in detail.

However, another useful tool that I use when it comes to decision making is to envision three circles. This creates a very useful and effective "decision-making matrix" that helps me balance the essential aspects of my life and identify the right actions to take. Using three circles also tends to avoid the either-or dilemmas that dualities often embody. Interestingly, many complex situations condense naturally and logically into three arenas. Perhaps three *is* a magic number. One that appears throughout this book is embodied by the three bricklayers: that is, self, others or family, and the world or spirituality.

Here is how this works in action. Whenever I am faced with a career question, or when I'm deciding whether or not to pursue or accept a new job, I envision a slightly different set of three circles: impact, joy, and financial sustainability (though you can redefine these areas to fit your situation or dilemma). The three questions I ask and answer are: 1.) Does my work have positive impact? 2.) Does my work bring joy to me and to others? 3.) Does my work provide financial sustainability?

These three categories can be seen as being in opposition to one another — more joy may lead to less impact and less money. A job that earns more money may lead to less joy. Ideally, I want a situation that elicits a positive answer to all three questions. I don't need each aspect to be literally equal. I'm not expecting perfect balance. At times I'm willing to sacrifice money and joy for impact. Often for me, however, impact is the most important. It's why I work. And yet, I also need to pay the bills, and without joy, what impact can I have?

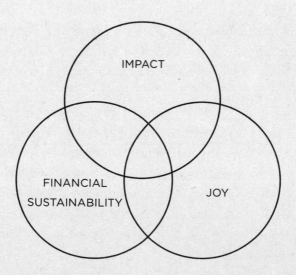

First, just applying these criteria shifts my focus away from fear, worry, and survival. Asking these questions shifts my attention from my day-to-day concerns to something larger: How do I want to show up? How do I want to live? Certainly, the answers I get may be vague, unsure. I may have genuine doubts and fears. Life is unstable and changeable, whether we're considering the economy, our relationships, or even our own feelings and dreams. There may be aspects to our situation that we can't, for the moment, change. And yet, where do we choose to put our attention? How do we find balance where there is imbalance?

Impact

Impact may mean helping one person, a team, a company, a community, or a nation. I remember once being upset when only six people registered for a workshop I was leading. I was hoping for at least ten people. When I mentioned this to my son, his response was, "Dad, even if you can positively impact the life of one person, isn't that enough?" I appreciated the sentiment, but to be honest, in the moment I wasn't sure. However, the workshop with six people turned out to be wonderful. A small community formed out of it and went on to meet several additional times over the course of the year.

The question of impact asks us to consider what role we want to play in our community and how our work serves others. By evaluating the type of impact a new job promises, we can try to assess: Is it the impact we want to make? Does it fit our talents and skills? Do we desire more impact than it offers? Will we be frustrated and discontent with this level and type of impact? Then, on balance, is the potential impact enough given our assessment of the other two circles?

Answering these questions prepares us to work effectively in the position we're taking. Yet this is also a question to pose regarding our current job. Particularly if you feel stuck in a position that, for financial or other reasons, you can't leave, ask yourself: How am I currently impacting others? How can I increase this impact in more satisfying ways? Sometimes, our current lives possess more potential than we realize. There are many ways, small and large, to positively impact others in our work. Sometimes our impact may not be seen or recognized outside of our company or department, or even outside of a particular relationship, and yet just listening, paying attention to one other person, can make a large difference. Have we become attached to making only one kind of impact? Maybe we want to run a company one day, but in the meantime, are we maximizing our potential as helpful employees, colleagues, mentors, managers, and so on? When considering impact, we should look at those we work with and those we serve, in addition to the good we hope our actions create.

Joy

We usually don't think of joy as being important in our work. Why is that? Most of us spend more time at work than any other place in our lives. Why not look for ways to bring a sense of lightness and enjoyment to what we do as employees or employers?

This criterion of joy also raises the question, What do you really like doing? What is nourishing, challenging, interesting to you? Is what you are currently doing aligned with the answers to these questions? What steps might you take to bring your work more in line with a sense of joy?

Thankfully, joy is the circle that is most within our control.

No job, no experience, is perpetually, continually, purely joyful; pain, difficulty, and impermanence will arise whatever our circumstances. Even a dream job will have its nightmare moments. So this question challenges us to find the joy within any and every situation. A certain type of joy exists in any job well done, and that satisfaction in accomplishment is often directly related to our self-confidence. Paying attention to and cultivating self-confidence can also be a way to cultivate more joy.

Financial Sustainability

Money and issues of financial stability are complex and personal. We all need to pay the bills, to earn enough income to meet our basic needs. This is no small matter. Indeed, sometimes this arena trumps all others: to earn what we need, to feed and house ourselves and our families, we have no choice but to take (or stay in) certain jobs. Considerations of joy and impact may seem like unaffordable luxuries in comparison.

As I've made clear above, however, the point of this three-circle exercise is to recognize imbalance and to identify actions to correct it. The first question within this criterion is simply, Does this job provide enough to meet my financial needs? If not, then joy and impact will certainly be lessened. However, that doesn't mean they need be nonexistent. In this case, our task is to create as much joy and impact as possible until we get our financial house in order.

To do this, we can ask another, larger question: What is financial sustainability for me? What is "enough"? If we are living beyond our means, then one answer is to adjust our lifestyle to fit our income. Would this be a better, more satisfying choice than taking a job solely because of its salary? Conversely, people sometimes make income-based work decisions with the belief that earning more money brings more joy and impact. Other times, people seek money as a response to fear or a desire for power. What purposes does money serve for you? Even if we are not in a position to change jobs, this is a question that deserves close examination.

Develop Your Action Plan: How to Work with This Book

The book is organized so that it follows a clear progression, but ultimately in this work, there is no first, last, or necessarily next step. This book doesn't describe a linear path to an endpoint. We each begin at whatever point we are at in this moment, and then we create our own unique path by walking it. Don't fall into the trap of thinking that you must finish one chapter or step before moving on to the next one, or that once you've worked through a certain paradox or step you will never need to return to it again. Rather, as with a tightrope walker, progress is measured by how well balanced we become, by how long and through what difficulties we are able to stay on the rope without falling, not in how far we travel.

Thus, this work inevitably entails a certain amount of experimenting and exploration, of trial and error. In my experience, some people are more comfortable with this than others, and nearly everyone learns more quickly and thoroughly when goals, objectives, and practices are stated up front. To help with this, I've designed Action Plan boxes that appear near the beginning of each of the five chapters in part 2. These Action Plan boxes list the hands-on practices and actions contained within each chapter, and each can be used like a discrete activity-based program for tackling that chapter's issues. Put all five of them together, and you have a program for the entire book. They condense the central teachings into what I hope you'll find to be a pragmatic set of succinct, cross-referenced instructions for helping to build a more fulfilling and meaningful life.

Some people also find visual analogies extremely helpful. You might explore thinking of this process like a circle, with each of the five paradoxes or truths in part 2 as points around the circumference of that circle. Further, each point in the circle is directly connected to all the others (see figure below). To move between and among them, there is no forward or backward, no beginning or end. Each pair of connecting points makes a necessary spoke in the wheel that is your life; in all likelihood, you'll traverse each spoke eventually. And just as there is no finish line, there is no stasis. In this work, we continually move between these points in whatever order and way is necessary to stay balanced, whole, inspired, and fulfilled.

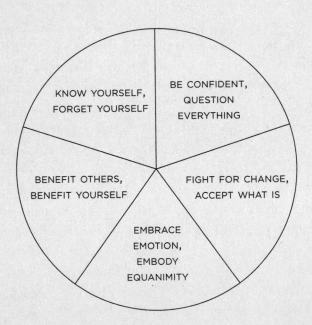

Those who like order and clear instructions can follow along chapter by chapter as though this were a step-by-step program. Those who chafe at rules and prefer to follow their intuition can pick and choose and jump around at will; the Action Plan boxes also make for handy indexes to quickly find particular practices and teaching stories (which will be described further in chapter 3).

Either way, and however you explore the material, notice what brings you alive and what elicits resistance. Pursue each of these feelings and notice what insights they may lead to. What do you learn? What can you unlearn? Be relaxed, curious, and alert; be confident and question everything; seek your own internal wisdom; and steadily hone the essential skill of knowing yourself and forgetting yourself.

Chapter 3

MORE CLEAR THAN CLEAR

All real living is meeting.
— MARTIN BUBER

There is a famous thirteenth-century story about Dogen, the founder of Zen in Japan. It is said that when he was nine years old he watched the smoke from incense burning at his mother's funeral rise into the air and disappear. The loss of his mother and the disappearing smoke prompted him to ask questions about life and death and how to live a profoundly meaningful and beneficial life. Despite his diligent search, he couldn't find anyone in all of Japan who could adequately answer his questions, so he ventured across the Sea of Japan to China, where Zen was flourishing at the time. He spent four years studying with a variety of accomplished Zen masters.

Upon his return from China, Dogen was asked, "What did you bring back from China to Japan?"

He said, "I came back empty-handed."

"Yes, but what did you learn?"

"Not much, except gentle-heartedness," he responded.

"Did you not learn anything else?"

"I learned that eyes are horizontal, nose is vertical."

Along with Dogen's interviewer, we are tempted to ask,

"Come again?" We expect that this great Zen teacher, the founder of Zen in Japan, will provide us with a profound teaching. Is this the sum of his insight? Emptiness, gentle-heartedness, and the shape of our face? His response is so simplistic it almost seems laughable, or else it seems deliberately designed to frustrate us, as if he doesn't *want* to give us the answer. But the story is sincerely intended as spiritual guidance, and though it appears almost too easy, it's not. Perhaps Dogen is telling us that the answers we seek are in plain sight. Much like our own nose and eyes, they are easy to take for granted and impossible for us to see directly.

No One Likes Paradox, but It's Useful

I'm not a philosopher. My interest is in change, insight, healing, and transformation; my job as an executive coach is to help people be more content, satisfied, and effective — solving real and important problems, small and large. My goal with this book isn't so much to understand Zen ideas or philosophy, but to create a practical guide to becoming more awake, more balanced, happier, and more effective. What I've found is that the Zen Buddhist approach to problem solving is, counterintuitively and paradoxically, particularly efficient and effective. In fact, many spiritual traditions, including Sufism, Hinduism, Buddhism, Islam, and the Desert Christian Fathers, have utilized paradox as a method for helping people to wake up, to be more alive, open, honest, creative. They use paradox to solve one of our most essential problems: as a bridge from the mundane activities of working, eating, defecating, and fornicating to the world of the sacred. Birth and death, self and no-self, here and not here, pain and loss — all are basic paradoxes of being alive, being human. We must walk a tightrope between them.

So, this chapter is devoted to exploring the basis or ground of Buddhist philosophy and its surprisingly effective approach to everyday life, and it also explains how to understand and work with Zen parables and the parables of our everyday lives, which I use throughout this book.

But first, what do I think Dogen was really saying? What do I think is the answer within his answer? Of course, there are many understandings. His simple statements reflect an entire worldview. One answer is that human life and consciousness are both clear and obvious as well as profound and mysterious. We are born empty-handed, and we will die empty-handed, and it is hubris to be too certain of what we "know"; this hubris leads to a narrow, one-sided view and ineffectiveness. Our minds want some assurance, some kind of map, something solid to hold on to, but we must let go of this desire and empty ourselves. Conversely, seeing only emptiness — getting stuck on the profound and mysterious — ignores what's obvious, what's right in front of our face: that we all share the same face, the same reality. Everyone is just like us, and kindness, gentle-heartedness, and compassion are never wrong actions. The Dalai Lama once proclaimed, "My true religion is kindness." In a world filled with difficulty, violence, poverty, and great disparity, perhaps gentle-heartedness is the only right and effective action we can ever be certain of.

Buddha Was an Effectiveness Teacher

Twenty-five hundred years ago the historical Buddha had an experience of awakening to the truth of how to live in reality with utter freedom. He was compelled to teach what he had learned. His initial and most primary teaching is referred to as the Four Noble Truths:

1. Being human contains difficulty. That is, there is no denying old age, sickness, and death.
2. Suffering is caused by grasping. That is, whatever our
   circumstances, it is wanting things to be other than they
   are that is the cause of our suffering.
3. Grasping can be transformed into satisfaction. We can
   change our relationship with difficult circumstances and
   free ourselves from suffering.
4. The way to do so is to engage in the following eight practices, which Buddha described as the Eightfold Path: Wise
   View, Wise Thinking, Wise Mindfulness, Wise Speech,
   Wise Action, Wise Livelihood, Wise Diligence, and Wise
   Concentration.

In the spirit of this book, here are the Four Noble Truths presented as two paradoxical statements.

First — Awakening is within suffering.
Second — We change the world when we change ourselves.

How are we to understand the Four Noble Truths and their
paradoxical nature? First, that both suffering and awakening exist,
and they are related. Change, impermanence, sickness, and death
are inherent to life and inescapable. All can lead to suffering. All
can also lead to awakening. It is the experience of suffering and
the failure of our desires to end suffering that lead us to pursue the
path of awakening. On this path, we change how we relate to the
world; we don't change the world or end the circumstances that
lead to suffering. By embracing suffering and accepting that the
nature of life is difficult, we can awaken and free ourselves from
suffering. This was and is a profound insight. Buddha's teaching

is to see and fully experience that within our suffering is freedom and happiness. Within our freedom and awakening is our difficulty and suffering. Embracing and living this insight is a lifelong practice.

Buddhism has been called the middle way, representing a path of moderation between the extremes of sensual indulgence and of asceticism or self-mortification, or between the physical and spiritual worlds. Though in the prologue I note that the term is sometimes misleading, the middle way is actually another definition for *balance* as I use it in this book: the most effective, awakened strategy is to ensure that none of the essential aspects of our life predominate or are ignored entirely.

A traditional story describes how the Buddha realized the meaning of the middle way when he sat by a river and heard a lute player in a passing boat and understood that the lute string must be tuned neither too tight nor too loose to produce a harmonious sound. This is completely aligned with a 2009 study showing that optimal performance is when effort is balanced, that is, in the middle between little or no effort and tremendous strain. Too little effort results in sleepiness or boredom. Too much effort results in strain and burnout. Making just the right level of effort leads to the best results.

Historically, the strand of philosophy and practices that became Zen Buddhism emerged in sixth-century China. During this time, the mystical, sacred practices of Buddhism in India merged with the practical, nature-oriented, farming culture of Chinese Taoism and ethically oriented Confucianism. Zen developed as a return to the practice of sitting meditation, with an emphasis away from philosophy and intellectual ideas. Instead, Zen focused on waking up to the ordinary and extraordinary experience of being a human being. The approach of Zen Buddhism is plain, simple, and direct, as well as mystical, complex, and profound: a paradox. All of Zen can be boiled down to three short statements: Do good. Avoid harm. Help others.

The Four Seals

Another primary focal point of Buddhist teaching is what are called the Four Seals of Buddhist practice. The word *seal* refers to a stamp used to make something official or significant. It is said that in order for a teaching to be considered Buddhist it must contain these four elements: difficulty or suffering, impermanence, no objective truth, and awakening.

For *awakening*, I often substitute three words: *freedom*, *intimacy*, and *clarity*. The word *awakening* is often translated as "enlightenment," and this can seem foreign and unattainable to most people. I believe that not only are freedom, intimacy, and clarity more useful terms, but they also more accurately represent the spirit and practice of people engaged in living as consciously as possible in the world of relationships.

I also like to add a fifth element to these foundational teachings, *reverence* — a feeling or attitude of deep respect, love, and awe, as for something sacred. These five elements are not beliefs. They are aspects or attributes of the Four Noble Truths. I like to think of them as a description of what is, of the essential factors in the lives of human beings. They are ways to see ourselves, others, and the world with more clarity, insight, and compassion. Here is a closer look at these "seals."

Difficulty

There is no avoiding difficulty in our lives. We are born, we will grow old (if we are lucky), and we will die. We will misunderstand

and be misunderstood. We will leave others and be left by others. We will be hurt by others, often unwittingly, and will in turn do our own share of hurting, by acts of either omission or commission. We can learn to accept, and to learn from, difficulty, especially in our relationships. Spiritual practice says, Don't try to avoid or escape difficult relationships. Don't try to escape pain or contradiction because both of these are unavoidable and can be great teachers. Keep exploring, entering, unfolding. Keep your heart open. Receive love when it blessedly comes your way, but be as supple and as understanding as possible when it eludes you or is even taken away. Surprisingly, to do so can make us happier or at least more at peace and less embittered.

Impermanence

Everything changes. There is nothing to hold on to. Impermanence is neither good nor bad. It is not an idea or a belief. It is what is. Who we are and who others are in this moment is different from who we will be and who others will be in the next moment. We see and experience change over long periods of time, but obviously changes are occurring in each moment.

No Objective Truth

Everything is interdependent. There is no objective truth. Everything that we think is solid is not — including ourselves, others, objects, even time. We live and breathe in relationship to others, and this very notion is fluid and subjective.

Within a personal context, I am young in relation to those older than me, and old in relation to those younger. I am a father and a son, a brother and husband. There is no little, unchanging person inside me directing my activities.

Within a business or organizational perspective, there are many truths. The sales team sees the world through different priorities and different eyes than the product development team and the finance team. I sometimes think that the book *Men Are from Mars, Women Are from Venus* could just as easily apply to business and corporate life: *Owners Are from Mars, Employees Are from Venus, Managers Are from Saturn.* These groups often see from completely different perspectives, all of which can be useful and correct. Our particular viewpoint, and its limitations, affects what we know and how we communicate.

Freedom, Intimacy, and Clarity

Experiencing freedom, intimacy, and clarity arises by accepting difficulty, embracing impermanence, and truly understanding that there is no objective truth. They are not some special stage or condition but a way of living your life in accordance with reality. It is living with a completely open heart, a completely open mind, moment by moment, situation by situation.

Reverence

Life is both mundane and amazing, perhaps beyond anything we can imagine. Since none of us knows how we were born or when we will die, reverence — a feeling of awe for that which is greater than us and beyond our descriptive abilities — is a profound and useful container through which to view and live our lives, and from which to engage in our relationships.

The Five Hindrances

Naturally, following the Buddhist path to awakening, or maintaining the effective balance this book advocates, is easier to understand than to accomplish. Why? Because we hinder and undermine ourselves. Buddhism speaks of the Five Hindrances. These represent the problems we have to contend with, or the paradoxes we have to solve, in order to live an effective life. Rather than thinking of these in negative terms, however, I suggest approaching them like tools. Working with these tools helps us to identify our self-destructive, unhelpful habits and to develop new ones. The Five Hindrances are grasping, aversion, laziness, excitement, and doubt.

Rather than single words, these are five broad categories that can help us identify our own particular fears and anxieties. One of my favorite lines from the Heart Sutra, one of the most often read and chanted texts in Buddhism, says, "Without any hindrances, no fears exist." All of these hindrances are addressed in detail in part 2, but here is a brief overview of what they entail.

Grasping is clinging, being caught by what we want. We all want things. Of itself, desire is not a problem — wanting friendship or to be competent or loved, for instance. Desire comes with the territory of being human. All humans have emotions, needs, and wants. But grasping is different from desire. Grasping is narrow and tight; it is inflexible. It holds. We grasp when we turn our need or desire into a story. We get hooked by our own story. In Tibetan Buddhism there is a word, *shenpa*, for this act, this process of a want or desire turning into grasping. We step into a thought pattern from our past or project a fear as we look into the future, and we hinder our connection with the present.

Aversion is the opposite of grasping, of clinging. It is turning away or avoiding. None of us like pain or difficulty. Not liking something is not a problem, just as desire is not a problem. Trying to avoid what we don't want or like causes problems. As when grasping, we can get hooked by the story of what we don't want. The story explains or justifies our aversion or places blame for our uncomfortable feelings outside of ourselves: "They make me uncomfortable," or, "It makes me angry when you say that." Feeling discomfort is just that, something we feel. Aversion is the story, the tightening, the pushing away (or the holding on to).

Excitement is when the mind is agitated, distracted. You can't sit still or focus. Excitement has come to be regarded as a positive quality in our culture. Our work is exciting, our vacations are exciting, our lives are exciting. Our lives are often so exciting that we risk missing our lives. The mind won't stop.

Laziness is not trying at all, not applying oneself, giving up, or simply giving in to one's desires and distractions. It's the urge to be comfortable in the face of difficulties. Of course, we all want to be comfortable, but laziness is a false sense of comfort and security. Laziness is losing sight of our own power, our values, and our vows and commitments to increase our awareness and to help others.

Doubt is a hindrance when it becomes skepticism and cynicism. It's when we say, Why bother? Nothing ever changes. I will always be this way. Others will always be this way. The world will always be like this. No one can know anything, so what good is it trying to be better or to help anyone?

The Five Hindrances are one way to look at our lives. Each of us could easily develop our own list of hindrances, and even different schools of Buddhism develop their own particular lists. The categories don't matter so much as recognizing when our thoughts and actions have led us astray from the Four Seals and the Four Noble Truths. What are your favorite hindrances? Which ones knock you out of balance most easily? Do you have three or five or ten hindrances that make you confused, that cause you to flail around and create more suffering for yourself? To be effective, we must come to know our own tendencies, for what is a hindrance for one person might be a breeze for the next, and so on.

Wash Your Bowl

The hindrances, all by themselves, are troublesome. Even worse, we often live our lives not realizing we are at their mercy. As I've said, one of the main purposes of Zen stories or parables is to wake us up to the self-defeating behaviors and assumptions we are living under. These stories are written to surprise, shock, confuse, and rattle our expectations. We are meant to ask: What does that mean? Sometimes we are also meant to laugh. Paradox, like tragedy, is often funny.

There is another famous Zen dialogue from ancient China about a monk and a teacher. The monk arrives at the monastery and says to the teacher, "I've arrived. Please give me your teaching."

The teacher says, "Have you eaten your breakfast?"

The monk responds, "Yes, I have."

The teacher says, "Wash your bowl."

The monk understood. What could be more obvious?

In Zen Buddhism, a story like this is known as a koan. Koans are not tests. You don't answer the questions they pose and move on. Koans are meant to be meditated on. They are used to deepen one's understanding, to transform the way in which one experiences one's own self and the world, generally by cutting through habits, patterns, and conventional views and attitudes. A koan doesn't necessarily have an answer, though it may have several answers or interpretations. One learns by staying with the question — or the paradox or conundrum the story represents — and developing a deeper understanding, seeing all the ways it applies, uncovering hidden places within one's consciousness, and developing one's ability to learn and grow. In this way, the teaching becomes a lived experience rather than remaining an intellectual understanding.

A student is meant to just repeat the story or koan while going for a walk or during meditation practice. The story can often be distilled into a single phrase: "Wash your bowl." During meditation or anytime, you can say this phrase to yourself during exhales, repeating it until you eventually let go of the words and just feel the phrase begin to merge with your breath. If you repeat the phrase to yourself during the day, you may notice it coming up spontaneously from time to time. The phrase may become a theme of your daily activity; it may begin to influence you, bringing your ordinary daily experiences to a deeper and more mysterious level.

The point is not to analyze the phrase but to keep chewing on it, living with it. Working with a phrase in this way, it is possible to widen our usual understanding of things. The phrase can open us to what matters most, what is truly important in our lives right now, in a way that can inform or surprise us. Something in our experience that we may have taken for granted might be totally transformed. Or the phrase may merely point out something to us that we hadn't noticed before. Practicing with a phrase in this way brings us closer to, deeper into, our lives, beyond our unexamined habits and notions.

In addition, Zen stories often are not meant to be taken literally. The circumstances of the story are metaphorical, allegorical. In a story, if someone asks, "Where are you going today?" they invariably mean something like, "Where are you really going in your life?" or, "Where are any of us going?" As in the Zen story that opened this chapter, the question "What did you bring back from China?" isn't about a specific, actual trip. It could be read to mean "What lesson can any human draw from life?"

Then again, sometimes the meaning is both literal and metaphorical. My guess is that "wash your bowl" has just such a multiple understanding. On a metaphorical level it says to the student, if you want to receive the teaching — that is, if you want to learn, if you want to broaden your vision, open your heart, or expand your understanding of yourself and the world — begin by paying attention to and bringing alive the simple, mundane activities of your life. No need to look elsewhere for life lessons. The teaching you seek, about meaning and connection, is right in front of you, in the midst of everyday activities. Let go of your preconceived ideas about where the real teachings are and pay attention to what is right in front of you. Go wash your bowl.

We each have the ability to bring mundane activities alive — through our attention, curiosity, and openness. This is what Zen stories encourage us to do, to be fully engaged in every moment. How is it that we don't see how alive everything really is, right in front of us? How often do we hold back from being truly alive and present, waiting for just the right situation, job, or relationship? How often are we doing one thing without paying attention, only as a means to get to the "real" work? We may think, If only things were different, then we would engage; once we do this unimportant thing, then we will get to the meaningful activities.

Activities are mundane only if we treat them that way. Everything we do can be an expression of our innermost wishes, dreams, and intentions — a way to connect with our true calling and a way to help others open to new possibilities — right in the midst of conversations, difficult and messy feelings, emails, phone calls, and meetings. But only if we awaken to that possibility.

My First Koan: Don't Piss Away Your Power

If we pay attention, we will find that our lives are filled with koans — tiny moments that sparkle like jewels and reverberate with complex, mysterious power. In fact, any of the myriad conversations that make up our lives can be seen and treated like Zen stories or koans — that is, statements or exchanges that are distilled, unpacked, internalized, and examined carefully until the lessons they hold have changed us, expanding our minds, honing our abilities and skills. Any moment in our life has this potential, if only we stop to consider it in a larger light. I work this way with my clients all the time. We don't need to enter a Zen monastery to put this approach into practice. We just need to pay attention to what's right in front of us.

For instance, when I was in my early twenties and a young student, practicing and studying Zen at the San Francisco Zen Center's Green Gulch Farm, an older woman Zen teacher of mine looked me in the eyes and said, "Marc, you have a way of pissing away your power."

I didn't know what to make of this. I was stunned at her directness, and I was puzzled. Was this a criticism or a compliment? I felt bad, wondering why and how I was not embracing and utilizing my power. At the same time I felt encouraged because I had no idea I had any power to piss away! I thought, Where and what is the power that she sees in me, and that I don't see? With whom and in what context? I suspected that this statement was intended as a gift — one human being looking at another, seeing and expressing what she believes is possible in the other person. Not measuring and comparing, but acknowledging an intrinsically positive quality. What she offered was both a compliment and a caution that said, "Look more deeply at yourself. Don't squander your gifts."

Though she probably didn't mean it this way, her statement has been a koan for me ever since. I've stayed with this statement, and kept coming back to it, over and over, for nearly thirty years. It is rarely a comfortable puzzle, but it is an extraordinarily useful one. What is my power? How do I express this power? How do I give away my power, and at what loss to me and to others? How do I help others to find and express their power? This, I have come to understand, is perhaps the most central challenge and promise I make in my practice as an executive coach and as a Zen teacher. I believe it is also a key component of being a parent, partner, coworker, friend — asking, How do we help others, be present for others, respond to others in a way that allows them to find and express their own power?

The question of power can be fraught in a business context, and it comes up often. I will discuss power in more detail in chapter 8, particularly *spiritual* power and how that translates into influence and effectiveness. For right now, though, it's enough to recognize that all the power you need to transform your life is within you right now. The questions you need to ask, the lessons you need to learn, the ways you need to improve, change, or strengthen: all these things exist right now inside you. All you need to call them forth are attention and sincerity. When we are frustrated, when we fail, we often throw away our experiences as useless. Instead, be deeply present for these experiences most of all. Treat them like koans. Meditate on them. These hold the keys to your power. Don't piss them away or squander your gifts.

Part 2

THE FIVE TRUTHS

Chapter 4

KNOW YOURSELF, FORGET YOURSELF

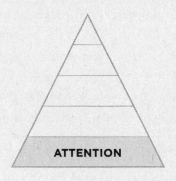

What is reality, after all?
Nothing but a collective hunch.

— JANE WAGNER

When I was in my midtwenties and living at the Zen Center's Green Gulch Farm, I had a teacher and mentor named Harry Roberts. Harry was trained by the Yurok Indians to be a shaman. He was also an agronomist, cowboy, and Irish curmudgeon. I was one of a group of students who helped take care of him during a phase of his life when he was aging and his health was failing. He taught me the proper way to cook chard (steamed with lots of butter) and how to drive his truck (using the brakes only when necessary in order to preserve them). He also taught me a good deal about confidence, about asking important questions, and about life. One day Harry said, "Being a human being is easy. You just need to ask and answer three questions. One, what do you want? Two, what do you have to do to get it? And three, can you pay the price?" A coy smile appeared on his face, followed by a loud belly laugh. "Real simple," he howled. "Very few people bother asking the first question!"

As you read this book and work with the material, notice any questions that arise for you. Ponder these questions, but don't be too quick to answer them. When a topic speaks to you, sit with it and explore it. For instance, this chapter instructs you to know yourself and to forget yourself. What does that mean to you? Is it liberating and deeply resonating or is it merely confusing? To which aspects of your life does it seem to apply? Do you struggle with either one?

I find that each of the central insights of part 2 contains a host of powerful questions, questions that open, provoke, and connect. These questions can sometimes have clear answers, but they are often multidimensional, paradoxical, contradictory, and changeable. How they land in you today may be quite different from how you worked with them previously. I'm surprised how often we don't ask the most basic questions — what do we want, what do we have to do to get it, and can we pay the price — in marriages, families, and the workplace. Of course, as I say this, I know why we don't just by looking inside myself: These questions can be tough to contemplate. We can resist them, and we may resist the difficult answers we find. Then we may struggle to apply these answers to ourselves, our relationships, and our work. As Harry said, real simple.

What's Your Story?

To me, knowing yourself means many things. It means understanding your personal likes and dislikes, your desires and fears, your skills, competencies, and learning styles. It includes knowing what you don't know, your blind spots, knowledge gaps, limits, and potentialities. In part, knowing yourself is intimately intertwined with your web of relationships; it's awareness of what others think of you and of your impact on others. Knowing yourself is being able to distinguish your story from reality, and it's knowing that you are the creator of your story. It is also, quite simply, your level of attention. How aware are you, in this moment, of everything going on inside of you and outside of you?

Forgetting yourself also means many things. It means the ability to be open to ideas and emotions outside of your own. It means being able to loosen and soften the particular ways you filter the world, which includes your understandings of yourself. It means seeing others free of your personal bias and helping others free of personal gain. It means feeling safe and comfortable enough to move into the unknown. It means the willingness to rewrite your story when necessary so that it better supports your success and effectiveness and the mutual satisfactions in your relationships.

For instance, a coaching client, Thomas, told me this story about a recent challenging situation he experienced with his wife of more than twenty years, Karen. After many years of avoidance and denial, they decided it was time to look carefully at their financial situation and to project as carefully as they could what their income and revenue sources might be as well as what their expenses and other possible expenditures might look like. I have sometimes heard therapists say that the two most difficult things for married couples to speak about openly are sex and money, with the difficulty being in that order.

Thomas and Karen had a frank discussion about getting

older, health care, and retirement. They talked about the kind of work they imagined themselves transitioning into as they neared retirement. As they looked ahead, they noticed that Thomas was generally more optimistic; he tended to see possibilities and opportunities. Karen was more cautious; she was quick to point out the risks and pitfalls. Significantly, they had a wealth of detailed information in front of them: the kitchen table was littered with spreadsheets and graphs of their current financial situation along with a number of future projections based on a variety of assumptions regarding different levels of income, expenses, and economic forecasts.

After several hours of examination, discussion, and debate, they came to a clear conclusion. Whatever happened in their old age, Thomas was going to be wealthy and happy. Karen was going to be poor and unhappy.

I couldn't help but laugh when I heard this story. It so vividly portrays the difficulty and barriers to relationships, to human communication. How is it that the same information can lead to such opposite reactions or conclusions? Little wonder that so many couples avoid discussing money (and sex), and why these most basic discussions of our mutual visions are avoided in the workplace. To talk about these issues so, we risk conflict that goes to the heart of who we think we are, how we see the world, and what we want. To even entertain the opposing viewpoint can seem to risk our own version of reality, our very self. This is no different in the political spectrum, where each side defines and defends its viewpoints in part by tearing down the other side, with little to no real engagement, listening, or meeting. How might things be different if we more skillfully asked the questions of what it means to know yourself and forget yourself? I believe it would make all the difference. These questions hold the keys to solving these types of problems and conflicts. Embracing, grappling with, and entering this paradox in each particular situation is how we achieve real meeting, real engagement, and real solutions.

I sometimes tell my coaching clients and workshop participants that we are so unique in how we think, process, and communicate it is as though we each live on our own planet. The mistake we make, the place where we get disappointed and experience lack of connection, is assuming that everyone lives on our planet. Then we try to convince others that, not only is our planet the best, but it is the only planet (even if we are not always so happy on this planet). Knowing yourself means knowing the ways in which we are all the same and the ways in which we are each unique, and using this to create open and productive relationships.

As you've probably noticed, we are much more inclined to perceive, feel, and cling to negative stories than to positive stories. Studies have demonstrated that negative events have significantly more impact on us than positive events. People will do more to avoid a loss than to acquire a comparable gain. Bad information carries more weight than good information. In relationships it takes about three positive interactions to overcome the effects of one negative interaction. In marriages, it typically takes five positive interactions to overcome the effects of a single negative interaction.

And from one perspective, this is all story. What you think about yourself, others, and the world is a story. Your views of success, of gaps, of how and why you need to change, all story. The changes you want to make in others — also story. The paradox? Story is important and real, and it is relative, multidimensional, and incomplete.

One of my guides and spiritual teachers often told me, in

relation to working out disagreements, disappointments, and anything else that was bothering me about my relationships with my coworkers, friends, children, and wife: "Drop the story!" She would say, "As long as you stay with your story, which is always one-sided, the outcome is clear and predictable. And it's not pretty. Drop your story, and many possibilities arise." She was adamant that there was no other way. I needed to take responsibility for the stories I told about myself and others. Similarly, to create a satisfying, happy life together in old age, Thomas and Karen will need to recognize and revise their financial stories. This won't happen if each insists on being right while convincing the other that he or she is wrong.

Know yourself, forget yourself, write your story.

KNOW YOURSELF, FORGET YOURSELF
ACTION PLAN

Knowing yourself (and forgetting yourself) is about paying attention. This chapter contains a host of varied practices for doing so in a number of different but important ways. Variety is good, as is persistence. Some are useful daily habits; some are yearly reviews. Try them all at least once.

1. Ask yourself, at least once a week: What do I want? What do I have to do to get it? Can I pay the price? (page 64)
2. Practice attention training (page 72) daily for fifteen to thirty minutes. Possible times: upon waking,

commuting to/from work, at lunch, going to/from meetings, after each phone call, before going to sleep.

3. Keep an attention ledger (page 78) once a week or month.

4. Journal as desired on directed topics (page 78). As a writing exercise, play the Game of Self (page 27) by answering your own question; or, do this exercise with a partner.

5. For serious conflicts, do the "opposite perspectives" exercise (page 80).

6. Conduct a personal audit (page 83) once or twice a year.

7. Practice letting go of a fixed identity (page 90) by dropping the story, stepping out of character, releasing anxiety, listening with empathy, and recognizing interdependence.

8. Use the hero's journey (page 96) to approach problem solving and conceive life goals. Journal regularly to monitor progress and write your story.

9. Take a moment, by creating monthly or yearly routines, to celebrate the return "home" (page 102) by acknowledging completed tasks and areas of growth.

KNOW YOURSELF

Who Are You?

One of the most famous dialogues from the Zen tradition is between Bodhidharma, a wandering monk from India, and Emperor

Wu, the emperor of all of China. Bodhidharma is a mythological figure who is often portrayed as a fierce, disheveled, wild character with bushy eyebrows and a scraggly beard. He is thought to be the founder of the Zen school during the sixth century, the first person to merge the mystical practice of India with the more nature-, harmony-, and farming-oriented Taoist tradition of China.

Apparently, Emperor Wu had heard great things about this wandering Zen monk, and a meeting was arranged. Upon meeting Bodhidharma, Emperor Wu asked him, "What is the highest meaning of the Holy Truths?" He wanted to know, right away, about the essence of Zen. Did it teach the secret of birth and death, of finding true composure?

Bodhidharma confidently answered, "Empty. Without holiness."

The emperor was stunned. He looked Bodhidharma in the eyes and asked, "Who is it that is facing me?"

Without hesitation, and perhaps with a bit of bravado, Bodhidharma responded, "I don't know." Bodhidharma then left immediately. When the emperor tried to get him to return, his assistants told him that this would not be possible.

This story is often used to describe the distinct flavor and attitude of Zen. First, there is the contrast between the wild and unvarnished monk Bodhidharma and the refined, wealthy, and powerful emperor. The story demonstrates the power of two worlds colliding and the Zen spirit of freedom and nonconformity. This conversation also contains an essential teaching of Zen philosophy. Though the emperor may have perceived that Bodhidharma was refusing to answer his question or to teach him anything, Bodhidarma's response was his teaching: Forget about holiness, just be yourself. Empty yourself of yourself, and pay attention to what is right in front of you. Stop seeing anything special. Find real freedom by being fully present in this moment.

Whether confused by or angry at this teaching, the emperor demands to know who Bodhidharma is. Perhaps his question is really, Who are you to imply that the emperor's status is meaningless? The monk then does something truly shocking. He continues his mode of teaching at the risk of his own reputation. He claims not to know himself and leaves. By his words and actions, Bodhidharma implies the meaning of the Holy Truths: that humans have no inherent, knowable self, and that you find real freedom by losing your fear of this unknown. Drop your ideas of looking good or looking bad, of right or wrong. Drop your story. Forget yourself.

In your own life, when the emperor asks, "Who are you?" what will you say? Knowing yourself is the practice of developing self-awareness, as well as the practice of mindfulness. Knowing yourself is having a good relationship with yourself, so you know your own emotions, fears, motivations, doubts, and aspirations. It also means knowing that we are always creating the story of who we are and recognizing the impermanent and ephemeral nature of this story. In this way, we become less identified with our ego, with our inner judge and our inner critic. We become less focused on, and less enamored of, the individual planet we've built for ourselves, and we become more fully alive, more fully present to everyone and everything that happens in each moment.

Dogen, the founder of Zen Buddhism in Japan during the thirteenth century, once said famously, "To study the Way is to study the self. To study the self is to forget the self. To forget the self is to be verified by all things." In the original Japanese, the word *study* actually means something closer to "to get accustomed with" or "to become intimate with." So what Dogen means is that as we become accustomed to the self, we see how changeable and ephemeral it really is, and we learn to forget it so that we might bring awareness and intimacy to all things — which includes ourselves, others, and all life. In other words, we move beyond the idea of subject and object, of self and other. In this context, Bodhidharma's response "I don't know" is not an expression of doubt, but a statement of fact. Bodhidharma could have described himself any number of ways, but these labels would have been nothing more than story. To get beyond story, you need to forget your story and practice mindfulness of the present moment.

Attention Training

"Let's do some attention training." I enjoy this portion of my workshops and seminars in the corporate world. Recently, when standing in front of fifteen CEOs of small and midsized companies, I began our session with these words. I continued, "I think you all understand the importance of attention. Your ability to focus in the midst of change. Your ability to bring your awareness to a variety of important business situations. And the importance of the quality of your attention, whether meeting with one person or your management team or standing in front of a room filled with employees and other stakeholders."

I could see that I had their attention!

The word *mindfulness* comes from the Pali word *sati*. Though *sati* is usually translated as "mindfulness," it also means "awareness or attention." A more literal translation of the word is "to remember." This primary concept in early Buddhist teachings is also becoming a primary concept in the practice of modern psychology. Mindfulness practice is currently being used successfully to treat anxiety in children and adults. It is even being used in the military to help soldiers to relax, to develop more confidence and flexibility, and to reduce the likelihood of post-traumatic stress syndrome, for it provides tools to deal with the unbelievable adversities of war.

Mindfulness practice, as defined by teacher and writer Jon Kabat-Zinn, is "paying attention, in a particular way, on purpose, in the present moment, nonjudgmentally." The psychologist Daniel Goleman says that self-awareness is the foundational skill of emotional intelligence, which he defines as "knowing one's internal states, preferences, resources, and intuitions." In essence, they are each talking about the same thing — attention, and the practice of developing our ability to focus and expand our awareness.

What is your relationship with yourself like? How do you relate to your feelings and emotions, to your inner voice of worry and fear, of love and aspiration? Is that a strange question — to ask about the quality of your relationship with yourself? Yet that relationship is critically important to how we relate to others, in the choices we make, and in how effective we are in the world. Attention training is mindfulness practice; it's a way of becoming more aware of your subtle and profound relationship with yourself. For the CEOs in my workshops, attention training promises the skill of getting out of your own way so that you can focus on the needs of the present moment. It's knowing yourself well enough that you can forget yourself when you need to.

Attention training is more than this, however. It involves a subtle yet profound shift in perspective, from self and the world of me to presence, to others, and to life. It is a shift from anxiety and ego-driven awareness to a wider, more inclusive, heart- and life-centered perspective. It is a shift from the thinking mind, the judging mind, and the scarcity- and fear-driven mind to just being aware, just being present. This shift brings greater freedom, flexibility, choice, and ultimately more effectiveness. Attention training fosters both a clearer and a kinder relationship with our thoughts, our emotions, and our selves, which is crucial in our ability to be present. Attention training brings more focus and greater appreciation — appreciation for life and for being alive. It brings greater depth, the depth that we discover our hearts have always been seeking. Developing this relationship allows us to increase our capacity for embracing paradox and opposing viewpoints. It is as though we have been seeing only in black-and-white and now we can see in color.

Attention training has four steps: setting intention, focusing attention, noticing distraction, and gaining insight.

Intention

There are many reasons to practice meditation, and in my workshops I often ask everyone to describe their intention to themselves. In general, I identify four large categories of intentions: well-being, stress relief, emotional intelligence, and expressing your true nature.

The intention of well-being is simply wanting to be healthier, more vibrant. You want to feel better, have more energy, be happier. You want to appreciate yourself, others, and your life. Those who are prone to stress describe an opposite but complementary reason: wanting to develop a strategy and practice for relieving and reducing stress in their life. They want to be calmer and more composed in the midst of demanding and difficult work and home lives. They may also want and need to sleep more and to improve the quality of their sleep.

Stable attention is the basis for developing emotional intelligence. Emotional intelligence is how we relate to ourselves and others. It is often defined as five broad areas: self-awareness, self-regulation, motivation, empathy, and social skills. The starting point for developing these attributes is attention training.

Beyond all these is a more mystical or spiritual intention for meditation and attention training. It is a belief that our true nature is kind, composed, and compassionate, and that we have inadvertently trained ourselves to be fearful, self-critical, and self-protective. If, through mindfulness and attention training, we can reduce or undo these limiting habits, then we can learn to express our true nature. Though avowedly spiritual, this expresses itself in quite practical ways. Just the act of stopping, of sitting without trying to get anything or change anything, can be seen as expressing your true nature. In this book's terms, it's the art and practice of knowing yourself and forgetting yourself, of being fully present, alert, and aware without being self-conscious.

Attention

Next, we begin the process of focusing our attention — on the breath and on the body, while noticing our thoughts and feelings, paying attention to all our sensations. I usually suggest using the breath as a focus point. I ask participants to shift their positions — however you are seated, change, even slightly, the way you are sitting. This is a way of bringing greater awareness to your body, and it signals that you are changing modes, shifting your attention.

In training ourselves to focus, we first bring our attention to our breath. Begin by just noticing that breathing is happening. There is an inhalation and an exhalation. If you want, you may count your breaths; counting exhales from one to ten, then counting inhales, is a useful way to bring some structure to the simple, and not-so-simple, practice of bringing attention to the breath. Or simply notice the sensation of the breath touching your nostrils, or the sensation of your chest and abdomen moving with each inhale and exhale. At the same time, start opening or expanding your awareness. This may seem like the opposite of focus, but it is just a different kind of focusing. Continue to keep your attention on the breath, and on the body, as you notice whatever arises — thoughts, sounds, tastes, sensations. Simply notice whatever arises, being curious and open, without becoming lost in these thoughts. The goal is not unlike that of the tightrope walker, balancing inner and outer awareness, becoming both performer and audience, neither predominating.

Distraction

However, you will be distracted. Thoughts or feelings will flood your consciousness; you will become lost in these thoughts and forget about your breath. When you notice that this has happened, simply bring your attention back to your breath. But be curious and notice: How easily do thoughts take over, so your attention wavers? How often does it happen, and how hard is it for you to return to awareness? Notice your emotional responses to these interruptions, these lapses. Are you critical and judging? Are you frustrated or angry? Or are you open and accepting? Can you practice "grandmother mind," the loving and caring attitude that accepts everything?

Oddly enough, distractions are essential to attention training. The idea is not to stop thinking, but to train your mind to control itself. By noticing your thoughts and bringing your attention back to your breath and body, you learn how to improve and increase your focus, and you learn how to expand your awareness beyond your thoughts. Through this process, you experience that your thoughts don't define you. Thoughts happen, breathing happens, sensations occur, and you observe them all simultaneously, aware and present, in the midst of constant change.

How amazing that this practice of attention training, just sitting, bringing your awareness to your breath and body, noticing distractions again and again, changes you, changes your ability to respond emotionally, even changes your brain. One study, done with workers in technology companies, demonstrated that practicing attention training for twenty minutes a day over an eight-week period leads to reduced stress, greater happiness (as measured in the brain), and greater resistance to the flu.

Insight

Several types of insights may occur during the practice of attention training. However, these insights may not concern the content of your thoughts or the way you think. One of the most important insights is that you are not your thoughts. You also may discover how busy your mind is. Through this practice, you learn how to bring attention to your breath and body so that there is less busyness in your thinking.

With attention training, you do not seek insight, and yet with the process of meditation you are changed. How is your thinking influenced? How is your body shaped? How do you bring this beingness, this nonjudgmental spirit, into your relationships, work, and daily life? Can you remember to pause during the day, particularly when faced with a difficult situation, and observe the state of your mind? Where is your attention? Are you lost in your thoughts, emotions, and reactions? Or are you calm, settled, curious?

In addition to using the breath and body as a focal point for your awareness during attention training, you may also experiment with bringing your attention to a phrase or question. Many of the Zen stories cited throughout this book can be used in this way. Phrases such as "Just don't know" and "Wash your bowl" are examples. Or there may be phrases or questions from your life that you can focus on, such as "What is my power?" or "What do I want?" The goal is neither to seek answers nor to look for anything. Bring your attention to the question or phrase in your mind; just stay with the question, pay attention to your breath, and see what arises. The paradox of insight is that there is nothing to search for. Just let go — of your story and the thoughts and habits that limit you.

Attention Ledger

The simple act of bringing attention to your level of attention is one way to improve your attention. In addition to mindfulness meditation, another way to do this is to periodically dedicate a day to keeping track of (by writing down) how well you're paying attention. On these days, keep a journal with you, and at least two times during the day, take a moment to evaluate and jot down your level of attention for each interaction or activity you've engaged in since the last time you wrote. Were you focused, present, clear? What were you doing, and what threw you off? These are meant to be quick assessments; just note the context and an evaluation of your focus. Then at the end of the day, spend some time reviewing what you wrote and reflecting on your day. Are there any patterns? Where do you need to pay more attention?

The main point is to build self-awareness, so that in the moment you remember to put your attention training into practice. Also, if you can identify situations that are particularly difficult for you, you can learn to anticipate and be ready for them.

However, for those who feel comfortable with it, regular journal writing is a very useful practice. Recent studies have shown that writing regularly leads to greater self-understanding and increased confidence. Experiment with more directed writing prompts, such as:

- What surprises me about my life right now is...
- What inspires me is...
- I feel most happy when...
- I feel least in balance when...
- What supports my well-being is...
- My deepest power comes from my belief that I...
- What I really want is...

Blind Spots: Seeing What You Don't See

The directive to know yourself is itself a paradox. As Bodhidharma implies, it's impossible. At least, impossible to know oneself fully, with 100 percent certainty. Humans are not made of stone; they change over time. Their perspective is also limited. We all have blind spots, and we will always have blind spots, even if their nature and size change as a result of our attention training.

So, to know yourself, pay a good deal of attention to your blind spots. Realize that things are occurring outside the range of your vision or senses or understanding. Continually try to see what you don't see. We instinctively know we need to do this, to uncover and understand our blind spots. We don't like blind spots. Eradicating literal blind spots has been instrumental in keeping us, our ancestors, and the human species alive. Not accounting for our blind spots leads to trouble — accidents happen when we don't see another car in our blind spot. Leaders are overthrown when they become blind to the negative effects of their rule. In the United States, the recent financial meltdown reflected a kind of societal blind spot. Climate change is a blind spot for much of the world. On a personal level, blind spots can lead to emotional meltdowns or surprising, often harmful actions.

Of course, blind spots encompass more than our limited perspective. Sometimes we *choose* not to see things. We avoid seeing the full (usually negative) impacts of our actions. We avoid acknowledging others who disagree with us; we overestimate or underestimate our abilities; and we fail to fully recognize our biases and habits — how we relate to stress, how we relate to the people and situations that trigger our emotions. This type of blind spot is often called our shadow, the negative aspect to an otherwise positive attribute or view of ourself. In this way, we write blind spots into the stories we tell about ourselves. We get married pledging to be faithful and abiding, knowing that most marriages end in divorce, and then find we avoid or censure any doubt, any difficulty, regarding the marriage we are in. As a spouse, we take pride in our good intentions, yet these blind us to how we might be self-defeatingly bringing to pass the very thing we would avoid. To the best of our ability, we must continually work to increase our awareness — to search out blind spots and look into the shadows — in order to increase our ability to create healthy, sustainable relationships.

In workshops, one way I demonstrate the power and limitations of story is with the following exercise, which helps to loosen and broaden our perspective and give us a glimpse of our blind spots. If you're alone, do this by writing. In workshops, I pair people up; if you want, find a willing friend or colleague. Decide who will go first (person A or person B). Person A begins by describing a real situation in his or her life that involves a significant difficulty or conflict; it should be a situation that is alive for the person now or from the recent past that still has emotional impact. Then tell the story to person B from two perspectives.

First, describe the situation as if whatever went wrong was all the other person's fault (or the fault of various other people). It was all them, 100 percent. Of course, you know this isn't true, but enter this feeling and attitude completely. Have fun with it; get into the role as much as possible. Then describe the same situation from the opposite perspective: the conflict was all your fault, 100 percent your doing. After playing both roles, what do you notice? Usually it is easy and freeing to ascribe fault and responsibility completely to another or to others. Taking full responsibility can be much more difficult, but trying this out can also be freeing — freeing of the burden of blame and of sticking to what is usually a partial and one-sided story.

The last part of this exercise is to describe the event a third time, this time from the perspective of wisdom: What would an outside person, someone who was totally uninvolved, have to say? How would a stranger describe this same event?

Literally speaking, seeing what we don't see is impossible. This is why I believe that knowing yourself is more an art than a science, and perhaps beyond both art and science. It is more of an intention, an attitude, and a way of being rather than a collection of facts, a personality profile we can complete, or a subject we can master. It is more like exploring the oceans or the cosmos than like getting your PhD degree. You never finish. The oceans and the cosmos are constantly changing and evolving. Just as you are constantly changing and evolving, the people around you are changing and evolving, and the circumstances you find yourself in are shifting even now.

PME Syndrome

In certain religious and spiritual communities, and in the self-help world in general, there is sometimes an outbreak of what I call

PME syndrome — premature enlightenment syndrome. After a time of intensive self-study, we tend to reach a conclusion that our work is done, complete. You know yourself. You can now kick back and relax. You've worked hard and seen some good results. Sometimes, on what used to be bad days, you notice that you are happy and less stressed. You feel a sense of accomplishment, even maturity.

However, humans are complicated. We can often be too quick to declare victory (in order to avoid the really hard work that awaits) or our small gains may themselves be a red flag. Are you happy and free from stress because your new-and-improved strategies for keeping stress at bay are well honed and well oiled? Or have you just become better at compartmentalizing? Are you simply more adept at keeping anxiety and difficulty in a little hidden box, while spending more time in a separate little box called "I'm feeling okay"?

For many years, particularly when I was young (though I still have to watch for this tendency), I sometimes used meditation and spiritual practice as a kind of safety net. I used them to avoid my own anger, and the depth of my own fear and self-doubt, rather than to see and solve them. One antidote for me, one way I upset and undid this self-defeating strategy, was to leave the Zen Center and go to business school in New York City. Starting and running my own business was a terrific wake-up call. If that wasn't enough to shake me from my habits of clinging to comfort and avoiding difficulty, I got married and had children.

Today, in addition to being an entrepreneur, I am also a Zen teacher, and I often remind my Zen students that the way we follow our spiritual practice today is perhaps more challenging and complex than what the historical Buddha attempted. He left his wife and children. He left the world of work and money. He taught that in order to walk the spiritual path, these were prerequisites. Yet we attempt to work, save money, own property, and have relationships, children, and families. The degree of difficulty for businesspeople exploring mindfulness practices — in order to live a more balanced life, one steeped in knowing ourselves and forgetting ourselves — is even more challenging. How foolish and how wonderful. Foolish because it is so difficult. And wonderful because of the courage it takes and the rewards that await those who persevere.

Personal Audit

You may want to conduct a personal audit, particularly when you want to bring more awareness to this work. I do this at least once a year and am often surprised by the results. Typically, it confirms changes I can be proud of while showing me other areas that still need focus, attention, and work. It is an excellent assessment when considering the self-care advice in the "Benefit Yourself" section of chapter 8 (page 242). It is a snapshot of your personal reality and health, blind spots and all.

A personal audit is easy to do. It takes less than ten minutes a day for ten days. Take a piece of paper, or create a form on your computer, laptop, or other recently invented electronic device. Write down these categories, and leave room for writing beneath each category.

- How much sleep did I get, and what was the quality of my sleep?
- How much exercise?
- How healthy was the food I ate?
- How much did I accomplish?
- What was the quality of my work?

- How many meaningful conversations did I have?
- What was my spiritual practice for the day?
- What was my general mood during the day?

Make ten copies of the form. Each day, answer as many questions as you can in the middle of the day, and finish filling out the form at the end of the day. At the end of ten days, take at least twenty to thirty minutes to look over your audit. What do you notice? Any patterns that surprise you? What did you learn? What could you do to improve the quality of your life?

Write down these impressions. If you wish, translate them into a series of goals for the next six months or year. Then, when you do your next personal audit, refer to them. This is, after all, how we track and confirm the progress of our business and financial health, and it works just as well for our personal well-being. It helps answer the dual question, Who are you, and how are you doing?

FORGET YOURSELF

Waking Up to Your Life

When I was twenty-six years old and living at the Zen Center's Green Gulch Farm, I received a phone call one day from my mother announcing that my father had been diagnosed with life-threatening cancer. The next day my girlfriend (who later became my wife) and I flew home to New Jersey to be with my father. When we arrived at the hospital, we discovered that no one had communicated to my father what was happening. We found him literally tied to his bed and highly drugged. My father had become so confused and disoriented from being in the hospital that he was wandering around the hospital halls at night. Drugs given by the doctor to sedate him seemed to have the opposite effect; they were agitating and confusing him further.

Fortunately, I had an excellent support system of colleagues back at the Zen Center, people who had a good deal of experience understanding how to work effectively with doctors and hospitals. My friends reminded me that I was in charge, that the doctors worked for me. They suggested that I have my father untied and stop all medications. They said I should stay with my father and communicate to him the truth of his condition.

After the drugs were stopped, it didn't take long for my father to return to close to normal consciousness. I had not been back to New Jersey in nearly a year, and for the past five years, since leaving home for the Zen Center, I had not spent much time with my father. I knew that my father was angry and disappointed that I had left college and was living at the Zen Center. I held my father's hand and we connected deeply. I told him what was happening, that he had cancer and the doctors did not believe it was treatable. His prognosis was that he might have weeks or months to live. I also told him that he should not give up hope. Nothing was certain. We cried together. He looked at me and told me that he was proud of me. He said that, though he had not been happy with my choices, he had now changed his mind. He was surprised and pleased with how I was now, in that moment. He said that he didn't understand what I was doing at the Zen Center, but whatever it was, the results pleased and impressed him. This may have been the most intimate meeting I had with my father during my lifetime.

My father asked me to hand him the telephone. He wanted to call his family and friends to express his love and to say good-bye. This came as quite a surprise to me. My father was extremely shy.

For most of his adult life, he expressed little emotion. He had been battling a manic-depressive condition and perhaps post-traumatic stress syndrome from his experiences in action during World War II. He generally repressed his emotions, including expressions of gratitude. Suddenly this changed dramatically.

A few days later, I suggested that we bring my father home to die. My mother was quite shocked. She had initially agreed that I should speak directly with my father about his condition, but she was in fact terrified by death. To her, the thought of his coming home was challenging. Still, she wanted him to be comfortable, and I committed to staying home and arranging hospice care for support. We brought my father home, and less than three months later, he died in my mother's arms in bed one evening. A few weeks later my girlfriend and I returned to the Zen Center.

It is sometimes said in the Zen tradition that practicing — studying yourself and forgetting yourself — is like walking in a gentle mist. If you just keep at it, you find, much to your surprise, that you are wet. I was not aware of changes in myself after five years of meditation, mindfulness, and devoting my life to studying myself. What a gift to meet my father in this way. And also, strange to say, what a gift his impending death turned out to be: through it, my father woke up to himself, to appreciating himself and his life and his entire family, and it unblocked the flow of love within him that had been blocked for so long.

What Forgetting Yourself Is Not

Knowing yourself and forgetting yourself are like two sides of a coin, as the saying goes. Perhaps more like two sides of your hand. You can look at the front of your hand and the back of your hand, and not only is it one hand, but where does the front end and the back begin?

Forgetting yourself would seem to be the opposite of knowing yourself, but it is really just another aspect of true insight, of real and effective knowing. However, since many people interpret "forgetting" in negative ways, it's useful to first define what forgetting yourself is not.

First of all, forgetting yourself is not unconsciousness in any form. When I first found my father in the hospital, he was so drugged he was unconscious to himself and his circumstances. He was not at peace; he was not effective. We are not meant to become numb to ourselves or to life. When Bodhidharma said that the Holy Truth was empty, he wasn't espousing nihilism. He wasn't saying everything is meaninglessness and there's no reason to try or care.

On the contrary, when my father emerged from his drug-induced confusion and found out the truth of his situation, he also emerged from a more insidious unconsciousness or forgetting: of trying to shut down his own pain, fear, and difficult emotions. Forgetting is not ignoring or closing off parts of ourselves we don't like or have trouble handling. This is only another form of unconsciousness. Instead, my father shed his negative ways of forgetting and embraced the most positive form. He put his impending death and his old self aside in order to express his love and gratitude for all the important people in his life. Facing death, he turned to soothe others.

In a similar, positive form of forgetting, my mother contained her own fears of death in order to make the end of her husband's life more comfortable. In the end, she accomplished this so well that she literally embraced death.

In more everyday terms, forgetting yourself is not dismissing yourself or undervaluing yourself in any way. It is not avoiding, denying, or suppressing. It is not about being forgotten, belittled, made small, insecure, or expendable. It's not about pissing away your power. Quite the opposite. When knowing ourselves and forgetting ourselves are in balance, we can act in service of others without ignoring our own needs. We can express gratitude for and value others without denigrating our own contributions. We are secure enough to see that we have an important role to play among many and that we can choose to play various roles.

Don't Forget, Let Go

In our daily experience, the idea and perception of me, I, and self is built into nearly everything we think, say, and do. It is built into our language — "I want a glass of water." Having a clear sense of self is crucial to our well-being, to our confidence and our relationships, and for nearly everything we do in this conventional world. And at the same time, it is useful and truthful to realize and understand that this idea we have about self is a convention; a useful, powerful, and compelling convention. Albert Einstein once said that past, present, and future are compelling conventions. As with time, so with self. As Buddha and many other wise people have understood, it is important to loosen and let go of the usual relationship and attachment we have to this idea of self.

Doing this requires a meta-cognition, an ability to step outside ourselves. This act alone requires a bit of not knowing. What is this awareness that can exist outside ourselves and allows us to see ourselves? Then, the more comfortable you become seeing yourself in this way, the safer you feel loosening your patterns and assumptions, changing your habits to fix your blind spots, and letting go of whatever doesn't serve you in this moment. All the aspects of yourself become less solidified, more malleable and flexible. Your sense of self becomes more like an improvisation, less like a statue.

Here are five ways in which forgetting yourself, relaxing your usual attachment to your sense of a fixed self, can be practiced and transformed into insight.

- We experience and embody the impermanence of life.
- We play with and explore our own patterns and stories.
- We let go of stress and anxiety and the identity that gets in the way of our effectiveness.
- We see from a variety of perspectives and listen with empathy and accuracy.
- We shift our perception from the world of me to the world of all of us.

Embodying Impermanence

As I've said, life is changing in every moment. We see this emphatically as children grow and develop, and when we stop to look in the mirror, we know it in ourselves as well. Yet we act as though beneath our skin is an operator who stays the same. Buddhism and science are clear that this is not the case, but all the same, we cultivate and protect this person, this identity or personality. We can learn to let this go.

By embodying impermanence, we give ourselves a gift of freedom. We recognize that who we are contains the element of choice, and in every moment, we can choose differently. Whatever we have done in the past does not preclude us from doing something different right now.

In some way our life resembles a river. Each moment the water is flowing, constantly changing. Some parts of the river are wide and move slowly. Other parts of the river are narrow and flow swiftly. The river bends and turns and changes, responding to the terrain and weather patterns. Yet it is one river. Seeing, feeling, and embodying this reality of change and impermanence in our own lives may be the most direct and powerful way to practice forgetting yourself. It is this type of forgetting that opens the door to our essential connection to people and to life itself, without boundaries, filled with possibilities.

Drop the Story

When my spiritual teacher once told me to "drop the story," this is what she meant: When you are caught in a story or a strong emotion, when you feel yourself tightening or your heart closing, just drop it. When a story or identity is causing conflict and pain, let it go as much as possible. It is not always easy. Letting go takes practice, so practice. Experiment with dropping the story. Drop it when breathing out. When driving, smile. When speaking in front of people, be a tightrope walker: present, alert, and relaxed.

If called to take center stage, do so to the best of your abilities; don't say, "No, I can't. I'm inherently shy and don't speak well in groups." If you habitually voice your opinion on every matter (no matter what conflicts this causes), or you habitually refrain from giving your opinion (perhaps to avoid all conflict), choose differently; step outside of your patterns and habits and find ways to skillfully participate as needed, meeting conflict or facilitating consensus as necessary. In my coaching practice I sometimes call this "stepping out of character." This is an important and practical skill.

If we are not too attached to our idea of a fixed self, then we have no fixed story: thus, as we evolve and change, so do our stories, particularly those about our past that "explain" who we are or why we are. This is another gift of freedom. Sometimes we get trapped by the stories we tell about ourselves, or by our interpretations of what past events mean. These stories create a ripple effect; if we believe them to be true, then we are influenced to live them out. But we don't have to do that. If it's true that we are afraid to speak in public, do we explain it by pointing to some humiliating event in childhood? Is that the story of our shyness? More to the point, do we use that story today to hold ourselves back? If so, then we need to work to rewrite this story. Nothing is set in stone. If we overcome our fear of public speaking, even a little, then the story of how we were made shy can also become the story of how we used that challenging childhood event to learn poise. What would happen if we told ourselves that story instead? One of my favorite greeting cards I published when I was CEO of Brush Dance said, "Fight for your limitations, and they are yours."

One way to loosen the sense of having a fixed identity is through meditation and mindfulness practice. Meditation is having a regular time to stop and experience that you are not your thoughts. Mindfulness practice is a way to bring more awareness and attention to your daily activities. This can be helpful in freeing yourself, especially from the stories that you create about yourself and others.

To be clear, I'm not saying that story is a bad thing or that we can eradicate stories. We think and speak and feel in the language of stories. When I say to drop the story, I mean stop holding on to that particular story; we don't stop being storytellers. However, we can utilize story instead of being pushed around by our stories. Stay with stories that support you and let go of stories that get in your way, especially stories that support and reinforce the idea of a fixed self.

Releasing Anxiety

Much of our anxiety has to do with our concern for and attachment to a primary identity, a sense of who we believe we are. The three primary qualities of self-identity are wanting to be good, wanting to be competent, and wanting to be loved. As I mentioned earlier, studies have shown that our attention is much more drawn to negative events than to positive events. As a result, our sense of identity is constantly being challenged; our efforts to be good, competent, and loved can feel like an uphill, sometimes impossible battle. This is the cause of substantial suffering and anxiety. I am quite familiar with this territory.

You can release this anxiety and loosen your sense of a fixed self by paying attention to the positive: noticing your innate goodness, and bringing attention to areas in which you are competent and where you are developing. Simultaneously, you can love yourself and also acknowledge the ways in which you don't fully allow or let in the love of others.

Seen in a positive light, the practice of forgetting yourself becomes generosity. Any authentic act of generosity is an expression of selflessness: you put aside yourself, your self-serving needs and emotions, to give others your time, attention, kindness, and love. So, to bring this insight to life in this context, practice generosity even with yourself. When you fail in some way, become distracted, or don't meet your standards, practice generosity rather than continuing to suffer anxiety and the judgment of your story.

Listening with Empathy

We live in many worlds, and without any effort experience ourselves and our surroundings from many viewpoints. We also tend to cling to one or a few viewpoints. We identify easily with labels.

We get hooked by the emotions of fear, desire, and hatred, and all the nuances of these emotions, which tighten and narrow us. Listening with empathy is a way to embrace paradox and multiple perspectives in order to see more clearly.

Empathy is the practice of feeling another person's feelings, while at the same time discerning that they are not our feelings. Thus, empathy is an active way we demonstrate both knowing ourselves and forgetting ourselves. We do this without any effort, yet we can also develop this as a practice. One simple, powerful method is to see all the ways you are the same as other people. Your desire to be good, competent, and loving is something you have in common with every other person. Your suffering, pain, and longing — these, too, are experienced by everyone. First, see how this is so for all those you know and love, and then extend this understanding to all the people in the world. Even those you may not like or are in conflict with suffer and want to be loved.

Recognizing Interdependence

Taking on the practice of knowing yourself and forgetting yourself is a subtle and powerful shift in how you approach your life. So often I see people searching for a calling, meaning, some direction in life that matters. I would suggest that this is it — the practice of knowing yourself and forgetting yourself. This is where meaning, where happiness, where waking up to what is right in front of you lies.

In practice, recognizing interdependence is what leads to our ethical code of conduct, or the rules and guidelines we use to determine the good and right thing to do. All societies and religions provide us with ethical guidelines. The three precepts of Zen Buddhism — do good, avoid harm, and help others — are simple, direct, and flexible. What actions we take to live up to them will differ in any particular situation, but as guidelines for our relationships and our work, they remind us to stay focused on how we impact others and the world of all of us. They require that we let go of our hardened and sometimes selfish views about ourselves, and they help us to open our hearts.

At Home in the Unknown

The path toward productivity, happiness, and effectiveness requires that we let go of our usual habits, patterns, and assumptions, that is, our fixed story. We make choices in each moment, either to trust ourselves to explore and to experiment, to change and to grow — or to stay with what is safe and predictable. Which we choose often depends on how comfortable we feel with the unknown.

It's easy enough to say, "Drop the story," but then what? Most of us have developed strategies for coping that work at least well enough to live the life we are living now. But to engage the central practice of knowing yourself and forgetting yourself — accepting and embodying that we have no fixed self — requires us to leave the comfort of our "home," the hard-won sense of self we have carefully tended up to now. Does that make you anxious? Rest assured, it doesn't happen in one great leap, like tossing your "self" off a cliff. In fact, it must take place in small ways, in our moment-to-moment choices, if it is to happen at all. Naturally and eventually, this comes to encompass a wider perspective and flexibility that guides the trajectory of our lives. We become more flexible: having insights about our past and present and using these to reshape our choices and direction as we move forward, in this and the next moment, and on through all the days and years of our lives.

But let's not kid ourselves: sitting with the unknown is never easy. We have committed ourselves to not knowing what will happen. We're improvising, risking, changing. Anxiety is inevitable, though it isn't unmanageable. That is one purpose of attention training: we learn to recognize anxiety and let it go before it drives us into the safety of our habitual self. We can, with practice, become so skillful at this that it becomes almost a reflex. Anxiety arises, we notice, and we let it go. And yet, even anxiety can serve a purpose: as performers will tell you, it sharpens your focus, gives you an edge, puts your senses on alert. Walk onto the wire or the stage without any nerves at all, and your performance is almost bound to flop.

To help us explore the unknown, and to take up residence there, if only briefly, we need a container for the experience. It's another paradox. This is, indeed, one very practical, effective offering of all the world's religions. They help teach us how to approach and enter the unknown and come back safely. This is certainly the purpose of the Eight-Fold Path of Buddhism, but it applies to Christianity, Judaism, Islam, and so on. I know I stand on the shoulders (and sit at the feet) of many thinkers from spiritual traditions, as well as from philosophy, psychology, and art, as I engage this topic.

However, in my executive counseling work, one container I've found particularly useful and effective is the hero's journey. This mythic archetype was made famous by mythologist Joseph Campbell in *The Hero with a Thousand Faces*, first published in 1949.

The "hero's journey" was Campbell's label for an archetypal, mythic pattern that he found emerged consistently throughout time and throughout the world's diverse cultures. This enduring human narrative provides a way for us to make sense and meaning out of the seemingly disconnected events of our life. In a way, it is almost like saying humans don't create their own stories; we all share the same story. Most significantly, Campbell saw the hero's journey as an explanation of how humans bring inner, spiritual truths into the everyday world. Like the Buddhist path, it describes a practical approach for creating an effective, balanced life.

Campbell identified seventeen phases or steps to the classic hero's journey, but the essential arc can be summarized as three stages.

1. Leaving the known and comfortable (often described as "home").
2. Entering the unknown and being tested or challenged.
3. Returning to the known (or home) transformed.

We are all heroes in our own journey, whether applying for a job; learning to play an instrument or to swim or to drive; embarking on a relationship; enduring periods of grief, or of physical or psychic pain; or experiencing times of accomplishment, celebration, and joy. The lens of the hero's journey can help us make sense of our lives, its critical moments, transitions, and overall arc, from birth to the approach of death. Ironically, paradoxically, using the hero's journey to successfully feel at home in our life's unknowns brings us full circle. It redeems that inescapable human impulse: to understand ourselves and the world, to find our place, to write our story.

WRITE YOUR STORY

Conceiving Your Hero's Journey

What is *your* hero's journey? How might you frame and describe your life in the terms of the hero's journey? Looking back, how might you describe your entire history from this perspective? Going forward, what journey lies before you? How might you describe your current work or personal situation, whatever you are setting out to do today or even in the next hour, as a hero's journey?

When I work with clients to consciously enter into the hero's journey, I typically emphasize seven steps or stages of the process. These aspects have the greatest resonance for me, and they seem most relevant to the issues in my clients' day-to-day lives. By engaging in this process, you can put the anxiety and challenge of the unknown, of knowing yourself and forgetting yourself, into a useful context and feel more expanded and effective in your life. You can feel clearer about each day's mission and your life's mission.

The seven stages are

1. THE CALLING
2. REFUSING THE CALL
3. GUIDES
4. TRIALS
5. POWER
6. INTEGRATION
7. RETURNING HOME

1. The Calling

The hero doesn't leave home for no reason. He or she is called to do something: to seek someone or something that is missing, perhaps, or because a person or event entices the protagonist away. This intention or calling is key: it sets in motion the particular challenges the hero will face.

What are you called to do? What project have you been putting off, waiting for the right moment to begin to think about it? What external problem or internal blockade is calling you to confront it, with courage and clarity? Bringing the question to a cosmic level, what is it you are called to do on this planet? What is your noble calling, at home, at work, in relationships, on your spiritual path? If you don't know, then how might you recognize or name the purpose of the work you are already doing? The nature of our purpose may reveal the nature of any difficulties we are facing. In addition, is there a personal quality you'd like to improve? Do you wish you could be more... loving, patient, artistic, organized, ambitious, attentive, generous, focused, serious, relaxed, happy-go-lucky, articulate?

Write down these callings. Craft simple statements of purpose or goals. You can have one or many, but each should be succinct, such as, "I want to be a more proactive leader," or "I want to start my own company," or "I'm called to change careers to become a teacher." Goals can be diffuse or concrete: to speak up more often at meetings, to be more emotionally open with family members, to improve your diet or exercise program. Whether you are already following this calling or just embarking, contemplate each statement like your own personal koan. Within each statement live questions, paradoxes, trials, and a journey.

Since what gets measured gets done, create your own journal for your particular journey. Use this during all the stages that follow. Make notes of progress and setbacks every day. Spend some time just reflecting on what the day has brought you in terms of your aspirations, and what your intention(s) may be for tomorrow. In real life, we don't always experience the stages of the hero's journey in linear order. As things happen, identify what stage they may belong to. Have you encountered a guide, received a trial? If it's not your style to write these things down, before going to sleep at night, think about these things. Do a mental assessment "balance" sheet.

2. Refusing the Call

Typically, the hero at first hesitates or refuses to leave on the journey. What are your fears and insecurities, your feelings of inadequacy? What reasons prevent you from setting forth? Or what is so attractive about home that you don't want to leave it, or are afraid you might lose it? I have had clients say things like "I don't have the time and energy to learn new leadership skills" or "I'm not happy in my current role, but it's a job." The most obvious and powerful reasons for refusing the call have to do with fear — fear of change and fear of the unknown. It can be difficult to let go of what is known and comfortable, even when we know we have outgrown our current situation. I can remember walking into the Brush Dance office one day, after being CEO for more than thirteen years, and thinking to myself, "My heart isn't here. This is no longer the place I belong." I was terrified. At first, I refused to hear this voice, this calling, that it was time for a change. In fact, I moved so slowly to pursue this calling that I was eventually kicked out before I could leave on my own terms.

Note that in the mythic stories not going is ultimately not an option. At some point, the hero must accept the call or else something of great value is jeopardized, often the hero's "home" itself.

3. Guides

The hero never succeeds alone. Finding friends, allies, and guides is an important part of the journey. These guides may point the hero in the correct direction, or pass along secret knowledge, or possess some skill the hero lacks. In your life right now, identify your guides and allies. What skills and knowledge do they possess that you need?

Significantly, the hero must ask for help. Guides typically do nothing until their aide is requested. Look at your list of people. How many have you specifically asked for help, or for help with your calling? Often, trusted friends or loved ones are eager to be asked for their opinion and expertise, but they may withhold until they are approached; perhaps they don't realize you need or want help. Sometimes, if you need particular skills, you have to hire someone's services; this is a form of asking. The hero sets out on the journey fully aware he or she is not adequately equipped for the task, and thus enlisting guides is critical. Examples of asking for guidance include working more closely with company supervisors or managers, finding a mentor, joining or creating a group that meets regularly (for social, community, or career reasons), or working with a coach or therapist.

In turn, you may be asked to be the guide for someone else on his or her journey. Think back: Has this already happened in your life? If so, how did you respond? Asking for help and helping others who ask sets up a virtuous circle of helpfulness and a mutual sharing of skills and encouragement. In truth, we are all guides for one another.

4. Trials

Once on the path, we encounter many difficulties, internal and external. We may uncover our own blind spots, limiting habits, expectations, and illusions. We may face difficult external circumstances, such as natural disasters, bad bosses, an unfriendly economy, other people's ambitions, and conflicts with those whose own goals and means for happiness obstruct our path. We may encounter issues with our own mental and physical health.

These can be real barriers and trials, but often they are more temporary than we assume.

5. *Power*

Through struggling with the trials, or some other key event, the hero's power is revealed. In Campbell's writing, this is sometimes depicted as a meeting being initiated by our father or mother: initiated into the world of adulthood, where we are able to receive the gifts and wisdom of our parents and simultaneously discover the wisdom and gifts that reside within us. Or, due to another event, such as a significant loss, change, or insight, we find ourselves coming into connection with divine wisdom and power.

In the business world I see many executives who find their own power in the midst of challenging situations. I believe this is one of the least understood and acknowledged gifts of the work world — the chance to move beyond what you thought was possible through working with seemingly impossible demands or seemingly impossible people.

Often one of the most creative ways to find your power is to identify how you give away your power. Explore this by writing (or by speaking with a trusted friend): "I give away my power when I...[say yes when I mean no; remain silent when I fear disagreement; and so on]." Then, explore the flip side. Write, "I find my power when I...[write without concern whether the writing is good or bad; speak clearly and gently when my feelings have been hurt; and so on]."

Sometimes finding your power can seem straightforward: facing difficulty rather than avoiding it, or using clear, direct, transparent language when stating what you want. Discovering your power is also a lifelong journey. Events continually challenge us, testing the core of our being. The time when I visited my father while he was dying was an enormous test and opportunity. I could have refused the call and not returned home, or I could have regressed into old familiar patterns in relation to my father. I felt misunderstood and not seen by him. Instead, by just being present with him, by meeting him fully where he was, my own power emerged, much to my surprise. Even more, my father saw and recognized this power, which I believe helped him to tap into his own power. In this moment, we helped each other and experienced a great gift.

6. Integration

Before returning home, the hero must develop ways to integrate the newly found wisdom and power into the ordinary world of work, family, and friends. You fully embrace the subjective nature of your experience and are aware and open to the experience of others. This can be accomplished through simple compassionate behavior, through stopping and really listening (often a surprising pleasure!), or through becoming a teacher or guide.

This can at times be more difficult than it sounds. I've seen business leaders make small and large changes in their ability to listen and be open, and yet these changes can be met with mistrust or suspicion from those around them. Integration can require skill, patience, and perseverance.

7. Returning Home

In the archetypal hero's journey, the hero is meant to return home, bringing back new, essential skills the community needs — such as improving our emotional intelligence or the ability to respond wisely and appropriately to challenging situations. We arrive "home" when we integrate and act upon what we have learned by following the initial, germinating "call" that beckoned us to leave home in the first place. In real life, completing a journey may take a few days or many, many years, and arriving home is more an acknowledgment of success rather than a physical return. We allow ourselves to feel proud, even as we continue to monitor and reflect on our journey. Ultimately, the hero's journey never ends, for we always need to grow as well as to guard against slipping back into ineffective ways of thinking and acting.

Life seems to move at such a quick pace these days that arriving home can easily go unnoticed. We fail to acknowledge growth and celebrate personal and professional development and success, while overfocusing on mistakes, letdowns, and all that remains undone. I find it useful, when working with coaching clients, to have a six-month development program, to set clear and measurable goals, and to acknowledge when these are achieved. You can do this yourself, creating your own program or enlisting the help of a coach or mentor (for more on this, see chapter 6).

At other times, change and growth can't be so easily measured or analyzed. If we pass a few trials, are we home or only partway on our journey? Unlike in the stories, satisfying endings can be hard to define. It takes time and attention, and sometimes quiet meditative space, to notice. Part of my returning home is to do a five-day or seven-day meditation retreat each year. This provides the time and the container to reflect, to notice, and to celebrate change, growth, and development, some of which I can name and some of which is more like a deep, unnameable stream within me. Do this for yourself at least once a year: take a day, or more, to return home and celebrate what you've accomplished. Contemplate and name your hero's journey. This is similar to the personal audit and yet significantly different: you are not just evaluating your health but writing and taking charge of your story, giving it meaning and shape.

I also find it helpful to use annual holidays and other community rituals to mark points of return and passages of time — for instance, each year I meet with eight men friends to connect, cook together, play, and help one another navigate our lives. Weddings and funerals make for powerful reminders about my own homecomings. And, of course, nothing marks our time more relentlessly than our birthdays (though some prefer to ignore these). For me, the process of writing is enormously helpful at any time to unearth the ways I am growing and finding my home. If you need a writing prompt, list the ways you've grown during this past year or the things you are most proud of. If you were hosting an event to celebrate your life during the past year, what would the theme be? In all these ways, and at all these times, ask: What does returning home look like in your life, from the perspective of your work, your family life, and your important relationships? What is your hero's journey, your home that you return to? How do you practice knowing yourself and forgetting yourself?

Chapter 5

BE CONFIDENT, QUESTION EVERYTHING

Whatever you can do or dream you can, begin it.
Boldness has genius, power, and magic in it.

— GOETHE

Only don't know.

— SEUNG SAHN, ZEN TEACHER

Many years ago, my mother was diagnosed as having an inoperable brain tumor, and we decided it was time for her to leave her home in southern Florida and to come live with me and my family in Northern California. At the time my children were twelve and eight. I was CEO of Brush Dance publishing company. I felt like not only a tightrope walker but a juggler as well — seeking possible treatments for my mother, coping with someone's terminal illness, running a business, being a husband and father, and helping my children face death for the first time.

After several months of visiting medical specialists and amassing many opinions, a pulmonary specialist detected that my mother had a severe lung infection, probably caused by the steroids she was taking to treat her tumor, which it turned out may not have actually existed. The doctor described a number of aggressive interventions to counteract this infection. When he finished, I was unsure and distraught. Was it worth the pain and suffering these interventions would cause? I took the doctor aside and asked, "What would you do if it was your mother?" Without hesitation he said he would take her home and help her be comfortable.

I described to my mother what the doctor said, and she replied unexpectedly, but with confidence, "I've lived a good and satisfying life. I'm ready to die." We discussed her options and made the difficult and emotional decision to take her home.

My wife and I set up our bedroom for my mother so that she could have privacy and a calm and quiet space. Yet the day we brought my mother home, she said she wanted to be where the activity was, in our living room, and she lay down on our living room couch. Was this wise? My wife and I weren't sure, but we agreed, and instantly my mother became the focal point of our household. Both my young son and daughter delighted in being around and helping to take care of their grandmother.

About five days later, late at night, my mother quietly and calmly breathed her last breath. My wife and I were with her, holding her hand, synchronizing our breathing with hers as much as possible. The next morning, I woke up my son, Jason, and told him what had happened. I suggested he stay home from school, and I was surprised and concerned when he insisted that he wanted to attend school. After the previous week, I felt certain the everyday concerns of the classroom were not appropriate for him. But rather than force the issue, I respected his choice. I drove him to middle school, where he was in seventh grade, and I returned home. About an hour later I received a phone call from Jason's school counselor. She said that Jason had been crying much of the morning and wanted to know if the school administration had permission to allow him to walk home. I said, of course. About thirty minutes later Jason arrived home; he entered slowly, with great presence and sadness. He looked at me and said, "Dad, walking is great in times like this. You should try it." We looked at each other, tears streaming from our eyes, and hugged for a long time.

Dealing with any terminal illness, any situation involving issues of life and death, puts us into a heightened realm where being confident and questioning everything are intimately entwined. Just taking the next step can seem to require a confidence we don't feel we possess — we aim to choose wisely and well amid quickly changing circumstances; we must be reliable, reassuring caregivers, pursuing treatments hopefully and with faith. At the same time, we question everything. We question, especially, the medical issues and decisions, the consequences of treatments, the emotional and spiritual issues of life and death, balancing work and family life and questioning how to best take care of ourselves in the midst of this.

In this situation, my wife and I had to question not only how best to care for my mother but the best way to care for our children. For them, would having my mother in our living room be inspiring or traumatizing? Should I have insisted that my son, Jason, stay home the day after his grandmother died? In the moment, I doubted myself, and yet I decided to trust his confidence and intuition, just as we respected my mother's choice to reside on our living room couch. Of course, in one sense, I was right that Jason didn't belong at school, which he himself soon realized. But only by leaving home did he find what he truly needed — a meditative activity in which to experience and process his loss and find some measure of peace with the unknowns of death. He returned from school transformed, carrying teachings and compassion for me. When we walk with confidence with our questions, we find blessings and answers we never expected.

BE CONFIDENT, QUESTION EVERYTHING ACTION PLAN

This chapter describes a way of being in the world. Every day, in any situation, we can practice these effective ways of moving through our lives and interacting with others.

1. Practice confident speech (page 113). Observe "left-hand column" judgments. Examine and rephrase word choice. Create positive stories.
2. Practice confident listening (page 116). Identify your part in any situation. Apologize for negative impacts. Ask for the opinions of others.
3. Be inspiring (page 118). Find "the juice" in every interaction and moment.
4. Incorporate "walking practice" into your everyday routine (page 122).
5. Practice the art of questioning (page 133): paraphrase, check your perceptions, set aside reactions, ask open-ended questions, and question yourself.
6. Avoid the "impostor syndrome" (page 135): acknowledge anxiety, use attention training, put aside limiting stories, and ask for help.

BE CONFIDENT

What Is Confidence?

It's a paradox, but it takes real confidence to ask open-ended, meaningful questions. It takes confidence to wonder and be curious, confidence to doubt and challenge your own thinking as well as the thinking of others. Acting confidently may appear to demonstrate that we know all we need to know, that we don't have any questions. But how often is this really the case? For life's truly difficult questions, we can never know all the answers. Can we be confident enough to move forward anyway, to stay with and admit what we don't know? It's possible to ask questions in ways that increase our self-confidence, and it's possible to act confidently in ways that undermine our effectiveness while also sowing doubt about ourselves. At first glance, the act and practice of asking questions may appear to be the opposite of confidence. Isn't questioning an expression of doubt? Isn't confidence an absence of uncertainty? But properly balanced, asking questions increases our knowledge and insight, which feeds our confidence to act decisively but appropriately given the unknowns, forming a "virtuous circle" — a healthy feedback loop of increasing confidence and insightful questioning.

There are many ways to describe confidence, though it sometimes goes by different names. Abraham Maslow described the abiding potential of human beings by coining the term *self-actualization*. This describes an essential confidence, encompassing a wide range of emotions; it's a person's ability to become more fully alive and more fully engaged. Peter Senge, in *The Fifth Discipline*, describes confidence from the perspective of "personal mastery." This is "approaching one's life as a creative work, living life from a creative as opposed to reactive viewpoint." This involves two essential movements: 1.) clarifying what is important to us, and 2.) seeing current reality more clearly. Senge describes personal mastery as a continual process of learning and growing. In other words, a life devoted to confidently questioning the essentials.

Spiritual traditions typically equate confidence with faith: a belief in the essential goodness of the universe and the unlimited potential of human beings, faith in a higher power or in our relationship with God. Like Buddha's path, this faith is as much a quest as an expression of belief: it is a movement from fear and suffering to enlightenment and awakening by following a combination of ethical and spiritual disciplines. In this understanding, faith is not freedom from doubt but what maintains us in the face of doubt. As in the story of my mother's dying, faith is trusting that the right thing will happen if we honor and respect our intuitions and best selves, even if we can't see the road ahead.

In business leadership, confidence and questioning are frequently described together. In his bestselling book *Good to Great*, Jim Collins describes the attributes of Level 5 leadership, the highest level of leadership, as being a combination of high achievement drive and humility. Achievement drive is having a vision of what you want and the confidence to decisively move toward it despite obstacles and challenges. Humility is the practice of not taking personal credit for success; rather, you give the credit for any success to the team and organization. Personal confidence is "balanced" by the recognition of group effort. Humility is an acknowledgment of our limits, of both understanding and power. It is a way we admit not knowing and keep ourselves asking the right questions, ones that widen our perspective.

In an interview with Charlie Rose, Ray Dalio — CEO of Bridgewater, a multibillion-dollar investment fund — described his business philosophy as seeing all new products and new business initiatives as hypotheses. Once you form a hypothesis, you act with confidence while at the same time questioning what will happen by listening, watching, and learning. He said, "It's not what I know that is important. It's worrying about what I don't know. I think this, but I may be wrong."

Dalio isn't satisfied with what he knows, but actively seeks what he doesn't. Daniel Goleman, in his writings on emotional intelligence, describes confidence in a similarly active way. It is a competence that can be developed, a skill. Within Goleman's emotional intelligence framework, confidence is having a strong sense of one's self-worth and capabilities by developing the courage to voice unpopular opinions, make decisions in the midst of uncertainty, and readily admit mistakes and change course as necessary.

Self-awareness is the first step in developing confidence. This includes cultivating strong emotional awareness — developing the ability to see emotions that you might habitually hide, even from yourself. To be able to trust your intuition and act with confidence when you are on the spot and in an uncertain environment, you attempt to recognize your own self-defeating thoughts and emotions and self-protective impulses. We act defensively to cover our weaknesses. So to avoid "defensiveness" (which often demonstrates a lack of confidence) we must explore and know our weaknesses intimately.

Once you do that, you can become willing and able to admit your own strengths and weaknesses honestly, to accept them, own them, reflect on them, and work on them.

The clarity of self-perception leads to self-honesty; that honesty enables accurate self-assessment. This clarity and honesty are what allow for confidence in the face of doubt. Eventually, you reach a point where you know you are not afraid to admit anything about yourself with anyone, even yourself. There is little about yourself you cannot handle. This is confidence.

Confident Leadership

When I first met Nadine, one of my coaching clients, she was confused and concerned. She had been a rising star in the corporate world and had developed a reputation as a dependable and creative leader as well as a trustworthy and accessible person. During the course of her career, she had assumed roles of greater and greater responsibility, from being a successful salesperson to managing a variety of teams. By the time we met, she was in her third year as vice president of sales in a two-hundred-person media company. Her team of twenty professionals consisted primarily of well-educated, dynamic salespeople.

Nadine expressed to me the same concerns that her company's CEO had conveyed — she was losing confidence in her ability to lead the team. Several team members had expressed to the CEO that they were not happy. There were differences of opinion regarding strategy, infighting among some key members, and a general lack of confidence in Nadine's ability to successfully lead this high-powered team. She had never before received less-than-stellar feedback from her boss and from her team. Nadine was beginning to lose trust in herself and was not confident that she could be successful in this role and situation.

Nadine's lack of trust reduced her ability to work effectively with important questions, some of which I raised during our first meeting. What did success look like in relation to her team? What did success look like in relation to her CEO? How would she know? What could be seen and measured? What limiting stories was she telling herself about her leadership ability? These were just a few questions to open up our conversations regarding confidence, effective questioning, building self-trust, and understanding the importance of how she framed her situation and what was possible.

Over the course of the next several months we worked on developing her ability to trust herself and to be more aware and present; we focused attention on her posture and her language. We worked on skills and competencies around presenting at meetings, communicating a clear vision, and heightening an atmosphere of team learning.

With Nadine, I worked on the following categories of personal and leadership development.

Trust and Speech

Lack of trust in oneself is the most common issue that I see in businesspeople as well as among nonprofit leaders across all industries. This is true of men and women, young and old. Anyone who is aware and honest has to work with issues of self-trust and self-doubt. Trust and confidence might sound synonymous, but it works well to think of them as a dynamic: trust looks inward and confidence projects outward. Attempting to appear confident without actually trusting yourself is empty. It can be seen through by others (and by you), and it makes you appear arrogant, foolish, or both.

When I worked with Nadine, we explored her habits and patterns around trust. Where did she have it and where did she lack it? One of the first things we did was bring more attention to her inner dialogue and her speech. Out of fear, Nadine had a tendency to overedit herself, so I encouraged her to be more expressive with her emotions and to be more explicit about her expectations of herself and of others.

Confidence can be reflected in how we speak. Confident speech is clear and sincere. It's more than just what we say, more than the information in our message. It's reflected in our word choice (how we frame our message) and our tone or timbre (how we feel about our message). When all these elements aren't aligned, it betrays a lack of trust or confidence in ourselves or in what we're saying.

To develop confident speech, explore bringing more attention to your voice and your language. Make every word count. Our speech is often on a kind of automatic pilot. We speak to fill space, without much thinking or consideration. Making every word count is a way of giving our words the weight that they deserve. Explore this as a practice. First, just notice the words you use and the way you speak. How do you talk and what words do you use in different situations? If a room grows silent, do you speak merely to fill up space? Do you speak tentatively in some situations and boldly in others? Do you "think out loud," figuring out what you mean to say as you say it? Begin to be more attentive to word choice, whether to express yourself, make a clear point, or skillfully ask a question. Make a conscious choice — every word counts.

Once she'd increased her awareness, I worked with Nadine on how she spoke to herself. We can display self-doubt, and erode trust, with the language that we use when we talk to or about ourselves. Here is a list of rephrasings I practiced with Nadine.

REDUCES SELF-TRUST	BUILDS SELF-TRUST
What if I fail?	What can I learn?
I don't know how.	What resources are required?
What if [a negative outcome] occurs?	Let's see what happens when...
I know what failure looks like.	What does success look like?
These actions appear ineffective.	What shifts need to happen to increase effectiveness?
I don't have enough power.	How do I tap into my power?

The words we use to describe ourselves are also clues to the stories that we tell about ourselves — especially judgments and fears. Nadine and I looked closely at her word choice to expose her hidden judgments; negative language tends to reveal negative stories. Sometimes this is called observing the "left-hand column," the thoughts that come up for us that we don't see but that influence our thinking, attitudes, and actions.

As we discussed in the preceding chapter, humans can't escape story. We create stories about ourselves and the world whether we want to or not. So let's bring awareness to our stories, positive and negative. Let's understand which ones lead us where we want to go and which inhibit, mislead, and betray us. Since we have a choice, let's create positive stories. Simply by paying attention to the words we use and the way we speak, we can rewrite our story into one that supports us, that reflects the present, responsive, resilient, and effective person we want to be. Like so many insights, it's a paradox: ultimately, our "stories" are not inherently real, but the way we tell them can help us to lead authentic, effective lives.

Presence and Listening

In practical terms, the more aware we are, the more decisive our actions become. But we only know what we choose to learn. To ease self-doubt and increase self-confidence, we need to ask: Where is my attention? Am I present? Am I listening well and asking the right questions? (For more on questions, see later in this chapter.)

With Nadine, I had her develop a mindfulness practice and a daily meditation practice. We practiced slowing down the busyness in her mind so she could more openly hear and listen to herself. This provided more calm, composure, and freedom, not only in her thinking but in her body. Our physical presence communicates the state of our inner lives even when we are silent.

We worked with her posture and physical presence, the way in which she carried herself, particularly when she was expressing her vision, as well as how she responded to difficulty and conflict. I helped her explore becoming more aware of how she used her hands, her head, and her entire body as she spoke. Her natural habit was to hold back, to keep herself from being completely visible and present. Just by relaxing and opening her shoulders and bringing awareness to holding her head up as she spoke and as she listened, she became both more relaxed and more confident. Awareness of her posture also made a difference in working with her team when there was conflict. Whereas her body language had previously been defensive or shrinking back, she was now more aware of both softening and staying present and engaged.

When it came to specific problems, I encouraged Nadine to ask herself, "What is my contribution to this situation?" This is almost always a useful question. It acknowledges your power, your influence and impact, as well as your limits. We are never merely observers, or innocent "victims," but neither are we fully in control. Defining our role is one way to ask the right question. It is not blaming yourself to acknowledge your part, whether positive or negative, in any situation. In fact, this is essential for seeing more widely and clearly, for finding the right solution and achieving the outcome that you want.

Then, when necessary, readily admit mistakes and failures. We demonstrate true confidence when we learn the fine art of apologizing, honestly and forthrightly. Especially when we unintentionally cause harm, sincerely saying "I apologize" shows we recognize our impact and hear the problems we've caused others. Similarly, being able to freely say, "I failed," or "I made a mistake," or "I didn't do what I said," displays resilient attention. That is, when it's followed with the important question: "What can I, and we, learn from this failure? How can I become more aware? What can I do better?"

These questions and acknowledgments display a true openness that is the heart of real listening and communication. They are the beginnings of conversations, not the end. Indeed, another important attribute is to develop the ability to have real and difficult conversations. When we become defensive (rather than confident), we tend to hold grudges, concretize judgments, and become cynical. Practice perseverance in the face of resistance, your own or others', and encourage honesty in others by being honest with yourself.

Most of all, mindfulness, presence, attention, and confidence are exhibited in how well we pay attention to others. Make a practice of inquiring about what others think and how they feel before assuming you know; before drawing conclusions, dismissing the opinions of others, or even dismissing your own opinions. It's a simple truth easily forgotten: effective leaders listen first and speak last. Then, you also demonstrate the quality of your listening, and your own self-confidence, by what you notice. Be humble and make a point to recognize the skills, strengths, successes, and good intentions of others. Build and honor these qualities among all those on your team, and problems will begin to solve themselves.

Vision and Inspiration

Nadine and I also worked on distinguishing between managing and leading. Managing is making sure everything gets done; leadership is deciding what gets done. Two key components of leadership are forming and expressing a vision and getting a group, whether that's a family or a board of directors, to express and agree on a collective vision. For Nadine, becoming a more confident leader meant stepping outside of and delegating some of her management activities, allowing her to spend more time strategizing, planning, and inquiring about the visions of others.

However, vision is more than developing an action plan. It's a way of seeing that brings each moment alive — each conversation, each meeting. In any situation, acting with a sense of vision means noticing your feelings and energy and moving toward aliveness — whatever that means. Conveying to others that sense of aliveness is how we inspire them to bring enthusiasm to all those boring but necessary everyday tasks. Conversely, we can learn to treat feeling less than fully alive as a red flag; it's a warning that inspiration is lacking and we need to pay closer attention.

There is a seventh-century Zen story I like to tell to illustrate this. A Zen teacher and his student went to a funeral to offer their condolences. They arrived early and no one was around. The student walked up to the coffin and hit it with his hand, then turned to his teacher and asked, "Alive or dead?"

The teacher responded, "I won't say alive. I won't say dead."

The student asked, "Why not?"

The teacher replied, "I won't say. I won't say."

Years later, after the teacher passed away, the student went to another Zen teacher and told him this story. The teacher said, "I'm not saying alive. I'm not saying dead."

The student asked, "Why not?"

The teacher said, "I won't say. I won't say."

At these words, the student had a significant insight.

Yes, it takes a spirit of serious playfulness to engage these Zen stories, which are frequently strange and perplexing. Are we meant to take this seriously? Imagine doing this: going to a funeral, rapping on the coffin, and questioning, alive or dead? What is the student referring to? Why hit the coffin? The action and the question are both upsetting and unnerving. And naturally, the Zen teacher will not say.

Whose funeral is it, anyway? My impression is that it is our own, and the teacher and student are standing over us, wondering: Are we alive to mystery, wonder, awe? Or are we dead to it? Are we open, aware, passionate, and daring, or are we closed, wooden, stiff, afraid? Are we willing to risk rapping the coffin and questioning the obvious? Can we see past surface appearances? This work, this relationship, this moment — alive or dead?

A question I like to ask, of both myself and those around me, is "Where is the juice?" Where is the energy, the risk, the edginess in any given moment? This is not about acting wild, or adding anything, but about uncovering what's already there, always. Have you developed habits and strategies that get in the way of feeling this spark, of seeing it in others? How do you breathe life into both important and mundane situations?

I won't say!

Buddhists Against Change

We want the world to make sense. We yearn for predictability. We resist and often despise what doesn't fit into our worldview, and we very much dislike change. I do. I sometimes joke that I'd like to form a support group called "Buddhists Against Change." Sure, acknowledging and embracing change is a foundational principle of Buddhist philosophy, but that doesn't make it fun or easy. As we develop our skills and experience, the last thing we want is to question our own hard-won knowledge, and yet we must. Life changes constantly. Attention training, mindfulness practice, and meditation are all methods of ensuring that not knowing informs our habitual approach to life, so that we don't succumb to the hubris of our assumptions. These practices help keep us from the trap of overconfidence, which is often a defense against the unpredictability of life.

In a 2011 *New York Times* story, Daniel Kahneman describes how wanting our ideas about the world to align with reality can lead to false assumptions. This issue came up when he was doing leadership assessment as part of his national service for the Israeli Army. His situation matches that of many executives I have worked with.

> After watching the candidates go through several such tests, we had to summarize our impressions of the soldiers' leadership abilities with a grade and determine who would be eligible for officer training.... We were completely confident in our evaluations and believed that what we saw pointed directly to the future.
>
> Because our impressions of how well each soldier performed were generally coherent and clear, our formal predictions were just as definite. We felt no need to question

our forecasts, moderate them or equivocate....As it turned out, despite our certainty about the potential of individual candidates, our forecasts were largely useless. The evidence was overwhelming....Our forecasts were better than blind guesses, but not by much.

I thought that what was happening to us was remarkable. The statistical evidence of our failure should have shaken our confidence in our judgments of particular candidates, but it did not. It should also have caused us to moderate our predictions, but it did not....We continued to feel and act as if each particular prediction was valid.

We are prone to think that the world is more regular and predictable than it really is, because our memory automatically and continuously maintains a story about what is going on, and because the rules of memory tend to make that story as coherent as possible and to suppress alternatives.

I coined the term "illusion of validity" because the confidence we had in judgments about individual soldiers was not affected by a statistical fact we knew to be true. The confidence you will experience in your future judgments will not be diminished by what you just read, even if you believe every word.

This is a wonderful example of how our desire for clarity can sometimes undermine our effectiveness — when we insist on order and clarity in the midst of complexity, the result is sometimes limited thinking and faulty conclusions about ourselves and the world. It's a negative example of how real clarity and confidence are often actually reached through embracing paradox, which can sometimes be more accurate and more clear than what we ordinarily think of as clarity.

Knowing and Unknowing: Walking Practice

My son, Jason, was right: walking is an excellent mindfulness practice. Done with attention and deliberation, it makes a very simple and accessible way to know and unknow, to undo and redo. Of course, we take walking completely for granted. I sometimes look at humans — who are generally five to six feet tall but who stand and move on two feet less than twelve inches long — and think how walking seems to defy the laws of physics. It is how the paradox of balance and imbalance becomes motion.

Do you remember learning to walk? Probably not. It happens when we are so young we don't have proper, adult memories. First you crawled, then little by little, you stood, wobbled, tested one step, fell, got up, and kept trying, over and over again. Gradually, with perhaps a few bruises along the way, you put it all together. You learned to really move and get somewhere, faster than you ever had before. Now walking requires no thought at all, like putting on your clothes. I remember taking an improv class in which we were asked to act out exactly how we get dressed in the morning. You get out of bed, and then what? Which leg do you lift first? What are your hands doing? Suddenly, by paying attention to it, the easiest thing became impossible: How *did* I get dressed? I couldn't remember. As I attempted to act this out in class, I had to admit that I seemed to know very little about how I put my clothes on! I was surprised at how asleep and unconscious I was to this simple daily activity. My body knows what to do, but my mind doesn't. My wife could show you better than I could, since she's watched me countless times. Walking and getting dressed, we shift into automatic pilot. Getting out of automatic pilot is exactly what mindfulness practice is all about, so what better way to do so than to unlearn and relearn how to walk?

I recently taught a group of forty employees at a major high-tech company the art and practice of walking meditation. This was in the context of an all-day mindfulness and emotional intelligence class. I demonstrated three different styles of walking meditation: In the first, a traditional slow-walking meditation, you take a half-step forward as you exhale, then shift your weight forward as you inhale. Then, you take a half-step forward with your other foot during the next exhale. With each single step, you complete a full breath. The second style is simply to walk at a slower-than-normal pace for about twenty or thirty steps, then turn around; as you do, you pay attention to your body and breath. The third style is to walk at a more normal pace and to deliberately shift your awareness: first focus on your breath and body, and then bring your awareness to your surroundings, and so on, back and forth, wherever you are. This third style can be done anywhere, and it is particularly useful during short breaks at work or in between activities.

After explaining the walking meditations, I mentioned a poem about walking by Nagarjuna, a first-century Indian philosopher. Nagarjuna wrote the poem intending to prove that walking, as we know it or think of it, does not exist. His aim was to deconstruct our assumptions, to get us off of automatic pilot, not only about walking but about any concepts about ourselves or our lives that we take for granted. We free ourselves when we dismantle our views. Where does walking happen? Nagarjuna sees even walking, like so many of our cherished assumptions and views of self, as a limiting, partial story.

Here are a few verses from the poem.

WALKING

by Nagarjuna, as translated by Stephen Batchelor
in *Verses from the Center*

I do not walk between
The step already taken
And the one I'm yet to take,
Which both are motionless.

Is walking not the motion
Between one step and the next?
What moves between them?
Could I not move as I walk?

If I move when I walk,
There would be two motions:
One moving me and one my feet —
Two of us stroll by…

Walking does not start
In steps taken or to come
Or in the act itself.
Where does it begin?

After they practiced walking meditation for twenty minutes, I asked everyone in the workshop to return and share their experiences. Several people reported that, as a result of the poem and their self-aware attention, they initially felt awkward, as though they had nearly forgotten how to walk! Yet they completely threw themselves into the exercise, as though walking for the first time. I responded with great enthusiasm. Excellent! This was the idea. When we let go of our ideas, we may feel awkward at first, but this increased awareness offers us new possibilities. We walk more skillfully, shedding unconscious assumptions that limit our effectiveness. If we would balance along this particular tightrope of confident questioning, we must learn how to walk all over again, loosening and letting go of those constricting habits that presume we live on solid ground.

Walk This Way

Here is another walking exercise that I occasionally bring into my leadership workshops (which I modified from an improv class). It is called "Walking with Confidence." Take a plastic water bottle, or any object about that size. Put it on the floor or ground. Move about twenty or twenty-five feet away from the bottle. (Yes, you need a fairly large and open, uncluttered space to do this exercise.) Stand for a moment, looking at the bottle on the other side of the room. Regard it carefully; visualize it internally. Now close your eyes. See it, still. Now, walk confidently, energetically across the room toward the bottle, eyes closed. Then — without slowing down — reach down to where you believe the bottle is and pick it up with one hand as you pass. If you are successful and pick up the bottle, everyone in the room should be asked to applaud you wildly. If you don't pick up the bottle, everyone in the room should be asked to applaud you wildly. In this exercise, the result does not matter. You are practicing visualizing, as well as walking with confidence. You are practicing confidence without knowing what will happen. This is the spirit and attitude you want to bring onstage if you are performing, and it is a great spirit to bring to any "performance" in your work and personal lives. However, please note: In this exercise, I always have a person standing on the far side of the bottle to act as a safety net, just in case the confident walker overshoots the target. There is much wisdom in the old expression "trust completely and always tie your camel."

In all these ways, experiment with paying special attention to how you walk. Try walking more slowly. What does it feel like to lift one foot off the ground, then to place your foot back on the ground? Where is the transition between balance and imbalance, movement and stillness, rising and falling, inhale and exhale, confidence and doubt? Practice not knowing how to walk, and practice walking with confidence.

QUESTION EVERYTHING

Not Knowing Is Most Intimate

In this ancient Zen story, one teacher is walking along the road and comes across another Zen teacher. The first teacher asks, "Where are you going?"

The second teacher responds, "I'm going on a pilgrimage."

The first teacher asks, "What is the purpose of pilgrimage?"

The other responds, "I don't know."

The first teacher concurs, "Not knowing is most intimate."

"Not knowing is most intimate" is one of the greatest teaching stories in all of Zen. Some teachers utilize this one phrase as the core of their teaching, repeating it over and over. It is surprising and puzzling and feels true, all at the same time.

Try this yourself. Take the phrase "Not knowing is most intimate," or just "not knowing," and repeat it while going for a walk or during your meditation practice. At any time throughout your day, say this phrase to yourself, letting go of the words themselves. Don't think too much about the phrase itself. Don't work it like a Rubik's Cube, puzzling out how to "solve" it. Simply keep chewing on it. Let the phrase merge with your breath, a reminder to bring your awareness to this moment, to open or widen your usual understandings. The phrase is like a flashlight showing us where to look, illuminating our unquestioned assumptions with "not knowing."

What does this story mean, and how might it influence your life? Like many Zen parables, the question "Where are you going?" is not meant to be taken literally. It asks, Where are you *really* going? Where are any of us going? Who are you? The response about going on a pilgrimage may or may not be understood literally. Whether the original story's teacher was on a pilgrimage is irrelevant. From a wider perspective, we are always on a pilgrimage — of birth and death, of living our lives, of deepening our practice by reducing suffering and confusion and increasing freedom and clarity, of knowing ourselves and forgetting ourselves.

The Zen teacher says, with apparent confidence, "I don't know," and the first teacher agrees. Thus, by its dialogue, rhythm, and nature, this story demonstrates confident not knowing. On a surface level of this story, the teachers appear ridiculous, but the point of the story is to look beneath or beyond everyday understandings, language, and ideas. What are we searching for? Why do we want what we want? What do we want to be and achieve? As when I'm asked, "How are you doing?" I often feel the real answer is either "How much time do you have?" or "I don't know."

In Zen, the word for "intimacy," as used here, may be a synonym for the words *awakening* and *enlightenment*. *Intimacy* is a word that is both more useful and perhaps more accurate to what the story is conveying. *Awakening* and *enlightenment* imply some special state of mind or spirit, some kind of transformative mystical knowledge or experience that somehow will bring us beyond life's day-to-day problems to a more spiritual plane. On the other hand, the word *intimacy* implies that we are becoming closer, less separate, deepening our relationship — with ourselves, with others, with the world. We are able to become more loving and trusting of ourselves and others.

This response "I don't know" pokes holes in our usual understanding and assumptions about knowing and not knowing. In conventional terms, to admit not knowing implies that there is something to know and you don't know it (and even further, that someone else does). That you don't know implies a criticism: you must be either stupid, or inexperienced, or mistaken, or lacking education. Further, by admitting this fault of ignorance, you must now learn what you don't know to feel good about yourself. Could valuing and embracing this dilemma of not knowing itself be the true purpose of pilgrimage — and an essential part of all transitions and an important part of life? This is difficult to admit to ourselves and to allow ourselves to fully enter and practice. Yet paradoxically, this is how we open, grow, and develop a deep and reliable trust.

The practice implied in this story is to embrace doubt and not knowing as universal, inescapable conditions, and acknowledge this freely. Instead of seeing not knowing as a fault, as representing some understanding we personally lack, we recognize that not knowing is at least one thing that we all share. None of us knows what will happen next. Since it is pervasive and universal, not knowing can be a source of connection and support in our lives.

Instead, our tendency is to show up to work or to our relationships as if we know. In a work context I sometimes refer to this attitude as putting on your game face — playing a role of confident assurance, knowing what to do and how to do it. In this way we defend our roles, our viewpoints and identities, at the expense of real confidence, real knowing. Everyday knowing is limited and can fool us. We think we know and see all, but like the board-carrying fellow, we see only part of the world. Our past experience points us in a certain direction, leads us toward a certain way of seeing ourselves and others. But who is this other person right in front of us — this student, this patient, this child, this spouse? How do we deal with this illness, this gift? Waking up, who do we see in the mirror? A child grown old? An adult who still is the child?

When I think about my most intimate relationships — with my wife, my children, my closest friends — they are alive not only because of what I love and admire about these people but also through this sense of how much I don't know. When I am paying close attention, I don't know what they will say or what they will do. I also don't quite know what I will say or do myself. Together, we create something that is alive, electric, and intimate. Some deeper mystery enlivens these relationships I "know" so well.

Can you let yourself be open? Can you allow yourself to be surprised by each new experience? Are you free enough to meet experience on its own terms? Can you feel safe and confident enough not to know? When I know, I can impose my experience and my viewpoint. When I don't know, I can learn from and be changed by each experience.

Not Knowing as Business Strategy

In the fall of 1989, I launched Brush Dance, which grew into a multimillion-dollar publishing company. From the outset, I was incredibly confident, and I had no idea what would happen. This dance of confidence and questioning accompanied every single important business decision I made.

I remember my initial inspiration: I wanted to make recycled paper, and products made from recycled paper, more accessible. I vividly remember the first time I gave voice to the idea. I was talking on the telephone to my good friend Steve Weintraub one evening, just after dinner. Simply describing this idea felt like a bold and vulnerable step. There was power in giving voice to the idea. Once I spoke it, I felt compelled to move forward, to take steps toward moving from an idea to creating products and connecting with customers.

But what did I *know?* I'd never run a business. I'd never manufactured paper. And there was no identified market for what I envisioned. As of 1989, no recycled-products industry yet existed. Availability and awareness of recycled paper were just coming onto the horizon. All I had was a passion for the mail-order business, having studied the industry in business school, and a belief that there might be a growing interest in recycled paper and environmentally friendly products.

And yet, only months later, I launched the company by sending out five thousand small catalogs (one page, folded in thirds) to a list of individuals. Brush Dance offered a collection of recycled-paper greeting cards and wrapping paper, most of which were graced with beautiful images painted and designed by my friend Mayumi Oda, an internationally known artist and a sincere Zen student whom I knew from my residency at Green Gulch Farm. I wrote a business plan describing our products, strategy, and financial projections for three years. I borrowed money from friends and family.

When orders for greeting cards and wrapping paper began to arrive in my mailbox, I thought, Amazing! People loved our products. We weren't profitable at this level of sales (first-year sales were less than nine thousand dollars), but I was encouraged.

The next year we sent out ten thousand larger catalogs (an eight-page, six-by-eight-inch catalog) to individuals. This time we added more cards and wrapping paper and some environmental games we had discovered. Again, orders flowed in. One day I answered the phone, and it was a buyer for Smith and Hawken, a garden-supply catalog and retail-store chain. They wanted to purchase approximately fifty thousand dollars' worth of our recycled wrapping paper. "No problem," I told the buyer. When I hung up the phone I nearly collapsed. "This is great! How will we do this? Who can produce this quantity of wrapping paper to meet their deadlines, and where will we get the funds?"

We also began to receive calls from stores wanting to sell our products, and representatives who were interested in selling our products to stores around the country began to contact us. I didn't know anything about the wholesale business. In fact, at the time, I didn't know what a representative was.

I also began to learn that people were purchasing our products not because they were made from recycled paper but because they liked the designs — mostly watercolor images with inspirational quotes.

Before the end of the second year of business, Brush Dance was evolving. Success was arriving faster than expected, in ways and for reasons I hadn't anticipated. We were transitioning from a mail-order environmental-products company to a wholesale company that made inspirational products. We remained committed to making environmentally friendly products, but that wasn't our selling point. Looking back, I see that this taught me the importance of having a clear vision while remaining extremely flexible and responsive. I moved forward with confidence, despite all the unknowns, and I embraced not knowing with a clear sense of curiosity, openness, and willingness to learn and change.

Brush Dance went on to become a leader in the cutting-edge inspirational and environmental-products industry, with worldwide distribution. Licenses included work by the Dalai Lama, Thich Nhat Hanh, Rumi, Yogi Berra, Santana, and Jerry Garcia. Yet every stage of growth included humbling, encouraging lessons in confident doubt, flexibility, and surprise.

I remember how confident I felt when I negotiated for the license to produce a journal to accompany the bestselling book *Care of the Soul* by Thomas Moore. This was several years after the book had been number one on the *New York Times* nonfiction bestseller list and had sold an enormous number of copies. I was convinced that we would sell a minimum of fifty thousand journals, perhaps many more. Fortunately, I respected not knowing and ordered what I considered an extremely cautious first print run of five thousand copies. The product was a complete failure. We sold less than three thousand copies in the first year, and we sold the remainder at a loss to a discount firm. Had I given in to my confidence, we could have lost much more. By remaining balanced, I stayed on the wire despite my stumble.

On the other hand, when we received permission to create a Thich Nhat Hanh journal, my hopes and projections were extremely limited. Yet this went on to become one of our bestselling products, year after year. Who could know?

I love business, and every successful business owner I know has stories like these. This is why I see business as such rich and fertile ground for personal and spiritual growth. How do we get stuff done in the midst of change — changing customers, changing competition, a changing environment? It takes tremendous, almost foolish confidence, along with a fool's ability to question everything.

The Art of Questioning

Most of us never received much education or training in the art of asking good questions. I didn't. In my executive coaching practice, skillful questioning is an important competence that I find I'm constantly developing, in myself and others. This skill is equally useful, and these same questions are equally applicable, in all aspects of our professional and personal lives.

The most important ability in the art of questioning is sincere caring and curiosity. This refers back to the previous insight, "know yourself, forget yourself." Asking questions that make a difference requires a level of presence. We deliberately, consciously put our own views aside and openly inquire and explore what others think and know. No amount of technique can take the place of sincerity and openness. Thus, it matters less how you phrase things than how you ask questions.

Then again, the types of questions you ask make a difference. Here are four different types of inquiry for others, and one for yourself. Become familiar with them, and practice using them. They are tools for understanding.

Paraphrase

Paraphrasing is simply restating what you have heard, being clear that you have gotten the key points of what has been said. This is similar to the practice of "looping," which I describe in *Less*: you repeat or loop back what you have heard someone say. As in, "If I understand you correctly, what I think you are saying is…"

Check Your Perceptions

Check to see if your perception is accurate. Rather than telling people what you know, ask if they agree with what you perceive.

"It looked to me as if you were uncomfortable at the meeting. Was my perception accurate?"

Set Aside Reactions

When you notice that you have an emotional reaction to something someone says, you momentarily set aside this reaction and feeling, the best that you can. You are not suppressing it; you notice it and choose not to react in that moment. Rather than getting caught up in your perspective, you remain curious about the other's thoughts and feelings.

As an example, it may appear to you that someone is not being honest or forthright about an issue. For some reason, he or she seems to be hiding something, perhaps true intentions or feelings. In yourself, you notice your own frustrations, hurt, and judgment arise over this. You put these aside for now and inquire, "I'd like to clarify something. I thought I heard you say x, and I'm curious as to why you said that." If you can sincerely put aside your own judgments and show genuine curiosity about the other, you can often create a safe environment for honesty.

Ask Open-Ended Questions

Open-ended questions are those free of preconceptions and bias. These are usually clear and direct questions with the intention of increasing understanding, both your understanding and that of the person you are speaking with. For example, "What happened during your meeting? What did you learn from doing that presentation? How was your conversation with Bob?"

Question Yourself

Learning to ask yourself questions and to work with questions can be a way to build self-confidence. Each of the five truths presented in this book can be formulated as a question for self-reflection. For example, What does "know yourself" mean to you, and how might you work with it during your day? What does "forget yourself" mean to you, and how might you work with it?

Some questions I often suggest that people work with in quiet spaces during the day are: What am I feeling? What is this life? What do I want? What is important to me? Am I doing anything extra?

Finally, here are two questions that are powerful in a work context but apply to any area of your life. The first is directed at yourself: "What does success look like — in my work, relationships, and other interests?" The second you pose to others: "What can I do to be more effective in my work, as part of our team, community, or family?" The more personal version of this question, which Zen teacher Thich Nhat Hanh suggests for partners, children, and family members, is, "Please tell me, how can I love you better?"

The Impostor Syndrome

I've missed more than nine thousand shots in my career.
I've lost almost three hundred games. Twenty-six times,
I've been trusted to take the game-winning shot and missed.
I've failed over and over and over again in my life.
And that is why I succeed.

— MICHAEL JORDAN

Recently, I was preparing to co-lead an emotional intelligence workshop for new employees at a major Silicon Valley tech company. My co-leader was Karen, a company human resources and leadership employee. We had never taught together before. As we were practicing, I could see that Karen seemed quite nervous and awkward. I asked her what was happening. She shared with me that she was terrified and feeling a tremendous lack of self-confidence. She often experienced tremendous anxiety speaking in front of groups, and here she was, not only speaking in front of a group, but teaching emotional intelligence. She wondered, fearfully, if a part of her was a charlatan. She wasn't sure she could go through with the training.

I looked at her and said, "We are doing this together. You are smart and an excellent trainer. I feel nervous, too, when I'm leading these workshops. I often fear they will not be successful or people will be disappointed because I haven't delivered on all their expectations. It is almost unavoidable to not have these fears beforehand. But since you will be teaching with me, I'm much more relaxed than if I were doing it alone. I know that you have my back. And you can relax because I'm co-leading with you. I have your back. If you forget something, I will jump in. I may not be the greatest trainer myself, but I'm skilled at making you look good. So relax. Let's have fun, enjoy ourselves, and teach important skills and materials. We are in this together."

In the middle of the workshop we began receiving great questions from the participants. They were clearly learning and engaged. While we were making the transition from Karen's presenting to my presenting, she and I made eye contact, smiled, remembered to each take a few deep breaths, and we relaxed and enjoyed our co-leading.

Every time I lead a workshop, it's a valuable opportunity to practice confidence and questioning in the midst of a challenging and meaningful situation. I've been in other situations where the outcome was not as pretty as this one. And yet, whatever the outcome, I'm nearly always surprised: what succeeds and what fails, what other people bring to the process and expect of me, rarely matches what I have anticipated.

This openness, this curious questioning of expectations and experience, is difficult to cultivate and quite different from the self-doubts Karen voiced, which everyone experiences. Having an inner critic seems to be a human condition, and rather than opening us to surprise and learning, it shuts us down. As opposed to the imbalance of overconfidence, this is questioning taken too far. Caution in unfamiliar circumstances is one thing, as is performance anxiety; fight-or-flight fears serve a positive role of keeping us out of immediate, life-threatening danger. Karen was not experiencing these things. She was caught up in a negative, critical view of herself, and for many of us, these negative views are reflexive limiting habits, a constant running stream of negative energy that limits and constricts presence, effectiveness, and joy. We are not taking an open-ended, questioning approach to life; we are questioning ourselves in ways that directly undermine our confidence right then.

It's strange. I've noticed in my own life how easily I tell the story of failure — all the things I've wanted to accomplish that I have not, listing all my weaknesses and limitations, cataloging my regrets. This seems to come more naturally than the opposite, though there's no reason I can't just as easily tell stories of great success and satisfaction — all that I have accomplished in my family, relationships, and work. When it's time for you to perform, which type of stories run through your mind?

Karen experienced what I call the impostor syndrome. People suffer this when they have not internalized their accomplishments, and they carry fear about being discovered as not deserving of their role or position. Secretly, they believe they are frauds. This condition flares up particularly in those moments when others turn to us for help and for the benefits of our experience.

In my coaching practice, and in my personal experience, it appears that most, if not all, people experience these feelings in some form; few are immune. Paradoxically, evidence suggests that this syndrome bears an inverse relationship to actual accomplishment. The more successful many people in business become, the more they harbor these feelings of being found out as impostors. It's as if they are hiding their "true self" behind a mask of effectiveness, power, and expertise, and it's only a matter of time before they are discovered as charlatans.

How do you escape this pain, this faulty questioning? The antidote isn't to ignore it, to keep acting a confidence you don't feel. Instead, become aware of it and recognize it as a limiting story you are telling yourself, a story of failure. Label this story, and know that there is another possibility called success, and more possibilities with names you don't know yet. Stories are just stories; they change and can be revised. Limiting stories of pain and failure can become stories of possibility — of learning and success and achievement. Which will you embody? What will happen? Wait, watch, listen, and find out. Don't dictate the habitual story you've rehearsed; be open to what comes.

In other words, to find balance when the impostor syndrome strikes, don't take your story too seriously or get too attached to it. Don't ignore this story; just put it aside. Focus instead on your body and breath. Practice attention training, breathe deeply and steadily, and bring your awareness into the present moment and what is actually happening. Then, shift your concerns from yourself and your role to your audience and their needs. What can you do to help them? Ask if you're unsure. Then focus on the task at hand, rather than your qualifications or skills, and simply do your best. Finally, don't be afraid to ask for help. This is ultimately what saved the day for Karen and me. Let others see that you're nervous, imperfect, and don't have all the answers. We can get trapped when we think we need to appear like the expert — perfect, without any doubts or questions.

One of my favorite Dalai Lama stories concerns an address he gave to an audience of more than three thousand people in Washington, DC. The Dalai Lama walked onto the stage, sat down, and settled himself in his chair. Instead of speaking, however, he began looking to his assistants, first to his right and then to his left. They all leapt from their chairs and ran off the stage. The Dalai Lama waited, looked around, sat silently. Then one of his assistants returned, stood in front of His Holiness, and slowly handed something to him. The Dalai Lama held up his eyeglasses for all to notice, looked at the audience, and said, "Anxiety."

In front of thousands of people, the Dalai Lama couldn't find his glasses, and this caused him to experience anxiety. He didn't panic, but he needed his glasses in order to read his notes. So he asked for and received the help he needed. Should he have pretended he didn't care, that he was above anxiety? He is the Dalai Lama, after all. No, instead, by sharing his anxiety with the audience, he used the situation to demonstrate a lesson in the universality of doubt, forgetfulness, and confident vulnerability.

Chapter 6

FIGHT FOR CHANGE, ACCEPT WHAT IS

*If you have these two things — the willingness to change,
and the acceptance of everything as it comes —
you will have all you need to work with.*

— Charlotte Selver

Last summer at Esalen I taught a workshop on accomplishing more by doing less for twenty people. These participants ran small businesses or were employees in small and large companies. I was leading them in explorations on reducing fears, assumptions, distractions, and resistance — perhaps another shorthand for how to become more effective in work and outside of work.

During one of our group discussions, the participants and I were talking about how to be most effective in business. I presented this question: "How do you respond to a particular need or challenge in growing or managing a business?" A few people responded that they act with a sense of composure, with a "whatever the Universe may bring me" mentality. They described this as their central belief about how to be effective in business and in life. They were probably thinking they were reinforcing a message of my workshop, since I am a Zen teacher as well as a businessman. Perhaps they were responding with language they thought I'd especially resonate with.

Hearing these words, I responded, "When it comes to growing or managing a business, I'm not a *whatever the Universe brings me* kind of guy. I'm a *write the f*#%ing business plan* kind of guy."

That got their attention. Accepting what is is an essential approach to life. But so is fighting for change. And if you want success in business — and in relationships, too, for that matter — then you need tenacity, focus, urgency, an intense achievement drive, and strategic planning.

FIGHT FOR CHANGE, ACCEPT WHAT IS ACTION PLAN

This chapter focuses on identifying and clarifying where you are in your life now, the gaps between your current situation and where you want to be, and creating a plan for bridging those gaps. At the same time the chapter offers tools and practices for developing more calm and ease by more fully accepting yourself.

1. Reflect on your life as if you were an orchestra leader (page 146). Write or consider:
   What are your current goals?
   What are you doing to realize them?

What skills are you already adept at, and where do you need more practice?

2. Practice cultivating spaciousness (page 148).
3. Do the "two eulogies" exercise (page 149).
4. Set your intention (page 151) by writing down all the ways you'd like to improve your life.
5. Identify your resistance (page 154) to pursuing these changes.
6. Measure the distance (page 157) of the creative gaps between where you are and where you want to be in terms of finances, joy, and impact.
7. Write a personal business plan (page 162) that converts all of this into measurable goals or steps along a specific timeline.
8. For one week, maintain a dual happiness index (page 166).
9. Now, every day, or anytime, do the "nothing lacking" practice (page 169).
10. Revise your personal business plan so that it includes scheduled laziness (page 170).

FIGHT FOR CHANGE

The Way-Seeking Mind

In the Zen tradition, the expression "the Way-seeking mind" refers to the decision to follow the path of waking up, of self-discovery, and of helping others. It is proactive, and sticking to it takes decisiveness, determination, and perseverance. It is also predicated on the need for change, within and without. Though it is not a path of self-improvement, the primary focus of change is oneself: shedding self-defeating habits and false beliefs (particularly self-gratifications, the seductions of wealth, fame, and comfort, and so on) to become more self-aware and thus more effective at driving change and improving the world. It is a path that embraces both change and acceptance, simultaneously. Accepting what is, by definition, creates the baseline for our understanding of reality and for our decisions about what needs to change. If we can't see reality, and can't accept what we see, then we'll never act effectively. Accepting whatever the universe brings can also be an important way to avoid wasting time and energy trying to change what cannot be changed. All by itself, though, accepting what is is not enough. The imbalanced, shadow side of acceptance is passivity, laziness, and avoidance. It is not leadership. If we see a window of opportunity and fail to jump through it, no one benefits.

On the other hand, the shadow side of fighting for change is becoming controlling and rigid in our concepts. In truth, our everyday lives are largely centered around coping with change: managing it, responding to it, and sometimes driving or creating it. To be effective requires knowing when to practice acceptance and when to drive change. This is more difficult than it sounds. Balance doesn't mean finding the middle ground between acceptance and drive. It means having the freedom, insight, and skill to embody both at once in order to act appropriately in each moment. To adjust continually and accept constantly. It is maddeningly challenging, yet simple, and forms the core of effectiveness.

Real change is at the heart of what it means to be human. With each change we learn and we re-create ourselves. We are able to see in a way that was not previously possible. We can act and achieve in a way that we could not before. With each change the world is different, our relationships are transformed. With each change we are continually expanding our ability to respond, to create, to envision, and to build our future. To clarify my terminology, the phrase "fight for change" could also be expressed as "lead to improve." That is, even as we accept that all things change, we recognize that many things can be improved, and so we take personal responsibility to actively pursue improvement. Thus, we don't simply wait for problems to arise and then try to solve them; we take the initiative to understand our current situation and envision a better future, a better now. We develop a vision, know where we mean to go, and start walking. This is leadership, and it is as vital to our personal lives as to our work lives. Indeed, they are intimately connected, and what "leading to improve" means in each can also be strikingly similar: seeing how we ourselves can be more open, honest, and effective, and exploring how we can better give of ourselves and bring out the best in others. Even as we consider the challenges, opportunities, and threats we will inevitably face, we can see that effectiveness rests in taking a balanced approach: anticipating that some problems will arise from within ourselves and some from without. Some challenges will require action, some patience. Some will need money and resources, some understanding.

It's mistaken to see our inner and outer worlds, our personal and work lives, our spiritual and community selves, as separate, disconnected. Zen provides useful, powerful tools and practices for solving real-world problems. Meanwhile, in pursuing strategies to improve our world, business can express our best selves and our most high-minded ideals — at all levels, by creating new products and services, by increasing prosperity, and by developing the talents and effectiveness of its own workforce. As we will

explore more fully in chapter 8, all these results can simultaneously benefit ourselves, our coworkers, and society at large. I
was recently on the board of directors of a nonprofit called Social
Venture Network. One of its vision statements is "changing the
way the world does business." Its mission is to change the underlying values and structure of business, so business isn't solely
defined as "maximizing shareholder wealth." The key is realizing, or remembering, that we are all shareholders. Each problem
we solve, each time we lead the fight for change on any level, we
all have a stake in success.

From Micromanager to Conductor

Tom is a coaching client in his midfifties who is CEO of a three-
hundred-person service company in San Francisco. He began
working in this company nearly thirty years ago. He has worked
hard his entire adult life. His company is surpassing its objectives,
and he has had a good deal of financial success. He is married
and has two teenage children. So much is working well in his life,
yet he acknowledges being a type A personality — ambitious,
driven, verging on being a workaholic (if not, at times, actually
being one). When we started working together, he told me he was
struggling. He was tired and burned-out. He wondered, "What's
next? What have I been missing, and is this all there is to life?"
He didn't want to work so relentlessly. He couldn't sustain the
pace anymore, and yet what would he do and who would he be
if he weren't working? He wanted to change his way of being.
He wanted to either take a sabbatical from his company or find
an alternative way to approach work. And he wanted to make
changes in how he approached and lived his life.

Our conversations began by assessing his work life now and
envisioning in concrete terms what and how he wanted to change.

One of my first questions was, "What brings you joy at your work now?" I also asked him how he got things done. How did he problem solve? What was the quality of his current work? So often, people only look at the "what" — the day-to-day activities, the tasks, meetings, emails, negotiations, and results. Some activities can appear immovable, but our perception of them can change depending on how we approach them. Ask yourself, How do I approach my work?

Tom's vision was twofold. He wanted to shift from being a full-time CEO to more of a chairman with his current company, and he wanted to identify his next big challenge, personally and professionally. In his company, Tom had assembled an excellent, talented, and committed management team. I also met with his team and was told they considered Tom a micromanager. Many of his managers had been with him for more than ten years and were quite capable of running the company. They admired and wanted Tom's vision, but they believed the company would operate more effectively if he were less hands-on. Since this was also what Tom wanted, the solution was clear: Tom just needed to change his management style, and then everyone would be happier, and the company might operate more successfully.

With a sense of pride, Tom described his current work approach. He was like a bulldog — relentless, driving, tight, and assertive. If this approach was appropriate and effective before, it was getting in his way now. I suggested he hold in mind a different image, that of an orchestra leader — not the person playing the instruments but the person directing the musicians from a slightly higher level. Conductors hold a clear vision and mission; they know the score. They also train and mentor the musicians. Sometimes the conductor is passionate and involved; other times he or she just sets the tone or maintains the rhythm. This persona, this new story, appealed to him, so we set to work.

I introduced Tom to meditation and mindfulness practice. He was, to put it mildly, skeptical. He resisted. "You want me to do what! Sit still for two minutes and follow my breath!" is just one example of his reactions. Yet, after a few months of daily practice, meditation became as routine as brushing his teeth. For over a year, we worked to shift habits he had learned over a lifetime — by slowing down the pace and developing awareness of his thoughts, his body, his emotions.

I also introduced the practice of cultivating spaciousness. I suggested that whenever he was feeling the anxiety of "not enough time and too much to do," he pause, bring his attention to his breath, and notice the space around him. Usually, all our focus and attention is on our tasks, other people, and objects. It is easy to feel tight, as if we lack the room to move or even to breathe. But what about the spaces that are in between? It is possible to bring attention to just noticing the amount of space that exists wherever you may be. Bringing attention to open areas, to what is in between, is a way to cultivate more spaciousness in the midst of our busy lives.

These practices facilitated the process of aligning Tom's intentions with his actions. Eventually, shifting this image and changing his activity made an enormous difference in his enjoyment of his work. This shift also catapulted the company to significantly greater achievements. Changing both *what* Tom did and *how* he worked increased his happiness and effectiveness.

As the quality of Tom's work life improved, it influenced the rest of his life. Previously, he would bring his work home with him, along with his hard-driving attitude. He began to relax more in other aspects of his life, including interactions with his wife and children. Spending time with friends and with hobbies became more important and more meaningful. In turn, our discussion of his next step turned more toward questions of his passions. What was his next big game? We used this term to describe how he might transform some of his hobbies into work that would benefit underserved populations or help relieve suffering in developing countries, whether that meant starting a social enterprise, running a nonprofit organization, or joining a nonprofit board of directors.

Today, Tom and I have been working together for more than two years, and the change has been transformational. It hasn't been easy, and it's far from over, but it's been immensely gratifying for both of us. It has been an ongoing lesson in how change and acceptance, intention and action, inner and outer awareness, when properly balanced, create a powerful, inspiring, creative momentum that changes us and our world.

When we look carefully at our lives, we see we are both conductor and musician. We decide what music to play, and then we must perform it using an entire orchestra's worth of instruments. Explore this for yourself. What do you see? In what ways are you leading? What music have you chosen to play, composed of what instruments? When you step into the pit, what is your role? What instruments do you play, and what do you need played around you? Where is more attention, training, or mentoring needed? Are there other players you can collaborate with to help make your concert a success?

Set Your Intention: Envision Success

I like to tell the true story of Roz Savage. This story is used in the motivation module of the Search Inside Yourself program that I helped develop and teach at Google. When she was thirty-three years old, Roz took a personal-growth workshop, and one of the explorations was to write her own eulogy from two perspectives:

one as though she would continue to live on the trajectory of her current life, and another as though she were to live the life she most deeply wanted. Roz began to weep as she wrote, realizing that she was bored and unhappy with her current life, with the safe choices she had made. It was as though in that moment she realized she was living someone else's life, not her own, and she understood what she really wanted to do. She wanted to do something physical and accomplish a lifelong dream that had been brewing and reoccurring in her heart. She wanted to row a boat across the Atlantic Ocean. After the workshop she left her job and redirected her life. Six months later she became the first woman to single-handedly row a boat across the Atlantic Ocean.

I applaud Roz Savage and the changes she made in her life. Certainly, writing these two eulogies is a great exercise, and I encourage you to try it. It is a powerful way to uncover the deep inner messages we have for ourselves about our lives and the choices we have made. However, the point of Roz's story isn't that you have to quit your job, drop everything, and do something spectacular to be fulfilled. The point is to become clear about what truly matters and what doesn't. Which dominates your life right now? Rap the coffin: Are you enlivened or deadened by what you are doing? I'm reminded of a few lines of poetry from David Whyte:

> Anything or anyone
> That does not bring you alive
> Is too small for you.

Whyte is not instructing us to be grandiose, to quit our boring jobs and our boring friends. Instead, he is asking, Why are you playing it safe? Why are you thinking small? Our constant challenge is not only how to dream big but how to embrace every incidental moment from the widest perspective. What do you really want? And how can you make the life you are living right now feel as fresh, inspiring, and alive as possible?

First, let's begin to answer some of these "what" questions; below we'll address "how."

Here are some basic questions to discover, explore, and quantify your intentions. Some may not apply to your situation; some you have likely considered before. However, as was the case with Tom, when we start to lose our way, it's vital to review the essentials. Our desires may have changed, and we need to set a new course, identify a new horizon. But most of all, identifying where we mean to go is the necessary first step in getting there.

I recommend writing your answers to these questions in a journal, though they can be just as fruitfully explored with a friend, coach, therapist, or small group of friends or colleagues. As you answer them, you will develop your own list of creative gaps — the projects you want to complete, the skills you want to learn, a business you hope to launch, a book that needs to be written, relationships you're seeking or hope to improve.

In no particular order, answer one or more of the following questions.

- If money weren't an issue — that is, if you had all the resources you needed — what would you do? What problems would you want to solve? What type of life would you lead?
- What kind of person do you want to be? What kind of partner, parent, child, sibling, human being? What personal qualities do you most admire in relationships? How

would you respond to the question, Who are you as a leader?

- Why are you here on this planet? Do you feel a larger sense of social purpose or calling?

- What do you wish you could do to make the world a more beautiful place? What everyday things, what huge things?

- In your current life, what problems do you wish you could solve? Be specific. If you want more money, space, or time, how much? If the problems are with or at work, what's your ideal scenario?

- In your current life, what would increase your joy? Do you play, laugh, and love as much as you want? What activities have you always wanted to do but haven't yet, or wish you could do more often?

Creative Gaps

Talking about, writing, and exploring our vision of what we truly want can be difficult, uncomfortable, and even painful. We become all too aware of the gap between where we are and where we want to be, and examining that distance takes courage, patience, and a good deal of support. Like the archetypal hero, we see our dreadful inadequacies and the world's insurmountable challenges and become afraid. We refuse the call:

"I would like to start a company, but I don't have…"

"I would like a new career, but I can't leave my job because…"

"I would like to be in a loving relationship, but it won't happen for me because I'm…"

"I would like to exercise, eat healthy food, meditate, travel [and so on], but I can't because…"

From where we stand right now, our goals, dreams, and visions may seem unrealistic or even impossible. "There's no way I can have what I really want because I've got a family to support. I don't have the resources." Our dreams can make us uncomfortable and uneasy, and so we may find ways not to dream.

We become vague, unclear with ourselves: "Oh, I don't really know what I want to do with my life."

We bury our heads: "I'm way too busy to think about what I really want to do."

We practice avoidance: "I'll do what I want when the kids are grown, the house is paid off, the recession is over."

We play it safe: "All I want is an easy life free of stress and worry."

But here we come upon a couple of hard truths and a paradox: One is, if we deny our passions, we can never be truly happy, and it will be difficult or impossible to find fulfillment. The other is, pursuing our dreams involves lots of stress and worry, and no matter how hard we try, we may never reach our ultimate goals. At least, not entirely or in the ways we imagine. However, strangely enough, if we follow the Way-seeking path, we won't be disappointed.

In my experience, when we honor the call and risk stepping into the gap, we enter a creative realm that changes us from the inside out. When we fight for change, we become changed, and there is literally no telling where that path will take us. Embracing this transformative effort becomes its own reward, and we sometimes prefer where it leads us to wherever it was we once thought we wanted to go. This is why I like to call the distance between our vision and our current situation a creative gap or a creative opening. And when it comes to creative openings, being uncomfortable and feeling tension are positive! Greet these feelings with enthusiasm! True creativity involves the discomfort, tension, and excitement of real risk. You are stretching yourself outside of your comfort zone, entering unknown terrain. Why do we feel discomfort and tension when giving a talk, leading a meeting, applying for a job? In all cases, it is like the tightrope walker: our vision turns to the possibility of falling, of failing. No one wants to fall or fail. The remedy for this is easy: just stay off the rope. But the price tag for this choice can be your growth and development, your happiness, even your soul. Accept where you are, make the changes necessary to move toward where you want to be, and slowly you will find yourself inching out and balancing successfully on that rope, sometimes unexpectedly failing, but then getting back up more skillfully.

Identify Your Resistance

When you feel tense and uncomfortable, examine those feelings; don't avoid them. These reactions can point to creative openings, and they can be used like alerts: "Ah, here is the Way-seeking path I was looking for!" Here are some ways avoidance arises and undermines our ability to take action.

- We don't have a clear picture of reality, of our current situation, and we are too uncomfortable to look closely and deeply. We allow this lack of clarity to stop us from taking action.
- We are stressed and fearful for no apparent reason. We suspect some kind of change is imminent. This is a creative opportunity waiting to be recognized.

- We feel unable or powerless to take successful action regarding the things we care about.
- We feel unworthy of what we want. We don't feel we deserve what we dream. Our fears of inadequacy keep us from learning new skills and competencies.

We also have numerous unhelpful coping strategies that keep us from clearly seeing and acting upon these creative openings. These are ways we minimize our uncomfortable feelings, to keep our fear of falling or failing at bay. If you notice any of these in your own life, use them as indications of something needing your attention: be curious and interested in feelings of discomfort. The best solution is often to face these resistances directly. Here are a few such self-defeating strategies that can prevent us from staying with our creative gaps.

LOW EXPECTATIONS: We may blunt our fears of failing by aiming low, as if failure will hurt less if we don't fall very far. This strategy often deadens our spirit and limits our growth. What do you learn by doing only what you already know how to do? What joy in success does that bring? Rather, don't always play it safe. Raise the rope higher, and try to stay on longer than you think you can manage.

ANXIOUS EXCITABILITY: In the face of a creative opportunity, we may get overwhelmed and come to believe that we need to create more anxiety in order to propel us to achieve our goals. I see this strategy used often in the business world — instead of dealing with the causes of problems, it can seem easier to be constantly putting out fires. Yet this strategy blocks our ability to focus on the real challenges and opportunities of the moment and will likely undermine our success. This can turn into the "I told you so" syndrome: we try, we fail, and then we say, "I told you I'd never succeed because I can't..." This type of anxiety is fear masquerading as excitement, and the cure is to calm down and breathe, put your emotions aside, and focus on the task at hand.

PUSHING THROUGH: This is another strategy I see often in the business world. When creative opportunities arise, our feelings of discomfort push us to work longer and harder. We hope, through relentless effort and sheer willpower, to jump the creative gap all in one go. Then we don't understand: "I worked so hard — how could I fail?" Quite possibly, we may be working too hard; our fear is causing us to strain and constrict. It is as if we are trying to run across the tightrope before learning to walk; we will lose our balance every time. In this case, the answer may be to relax, proceed more slowly, and pause occasionally to ensure that fear isn't driving us to rush.

It's also worth noting that not all anxiety and excitement are the same, even on a physical level. When we act outside of our comfort zone, when we agree to embrace a new task or creative opening, adrenaline courses throughout our body. We may feel pushed and uncomfortable in a way that opens us, stretches us. This is healthy and enlivening; it keeps us balanced on the edge of our seat. It actually improves our focus in the moment. This is the opposite of emotional stress, tension, and fear, which cause cortisol to course throughout our body. This fight-or-flight reaction causes us to constrict and tighten, and too much cortisol can lead to hypertension and is related to heart disease.

This is another reason to take a closer look at our moments of anxiety and excitement when they occur. Either way, they point to creative gaps, but are we approaching these fearfully (and self-defeatingly) or are we approaching them willingly, eagerly? In part, our own health is at stake.

Measure the Distance

Once you've verbalized your dreams — your destination, the place you mean to go — and once you recognize your habitual fear responses (so that you can skillfully work with them), the next task is to take stock of your current situation and measure the distance of the gap between where you are and where you want to be. *How* will you actually create the changes you want?

To begin, check in with yourself about your life and level of satisfaction right now. Conduct a personal audit, as described in chapter 4 (page 83), but do so with more detail and depth. Your current situation is nearly always more complex and nuanced than you imagine, and any serious goal will likely affect all aspects of your life.

In chapter 2, I described three circles I use for deciding whether to pursue a particular job or work path. These same three "buckets" — impact, joy, and finances — can be effectively used to clarify your current situation. They create an expanded personal audit, a way to take stock of where you are now and get a clearer view of your creative gaps. For this assessment, let's reverse the order. As in writing a business plan, I like to begin with what is easiest to measure — money — which is also often the most difficult topic to face and grapple with head-on.

As you explore and quantify where you are now, the particular shape of the creative gap will become clearer. Articulating this is how we figure out what specific steps to take. Any large goal will impact our whole lives, and it can be achieved only through numerous smaller goals, stages, and qualities. Measuring the gap is about identifying these things as well, so that we can take the most effective and efficient actions.

The practice of change and acceptance is a dynamic process. Producing the results we want requires that we proactively set out on a path and skillfully move toward accomplishing our vision. We do this by seeing as clearly as possible, developing a plan, and then being responsive and flexible to the changes and challenges that unfold along the way.

YOUR FINANCIAL SNAPSHOT

A profit-and-loss statement and a balance sheet are essential tools for running a business, and they are useful tools for understanding your current situation. What is your current financial picture? For most of us, this is very basic stuff, and yet I'm often surprised how many people don't create these tools, in either their business or personal life, or both. However, as you do this, pay attention to more than the numbers on the page; notice your entire self — your breathing, your emotions, your assumptions, and your stories. As you take a financial snapshot and create financial projections, does your breathing change? What emotions arise? Do you notice any loosening or tightening in your jaw, stomach, or back? Just notice. What attitudes arise; what stories do you tell yourself? In this way we bring our financial lives more in alignment with our deepest intentions and motivations.

On a few pieces of paper or a computer spreadsheet, create a profit-and-loss statement, a balance sheet, and a projected profit-and-loss statement or budget for the next twelve months. Do this for your personal finances and, if applicable, for your business.

A balance sheet is sometimes defined as a snapshot of your financial situation. In one column, list your assets: How much money have you saved, and what properties and things do you own? In another column, list your debts: What do you owe to banks, credit card companies, and others? Compare these columns. What is the reality of your current situation?

Then, create a profit-and-loss statement for the past year or the past several months. A profit-and-loss compares your income with your expenses; in contrast to a balance sheet, it describes where money is coming from and what you're spending it on. Start by listing all your revenue sources and totals. Then list your expenses. For most of us, calculating expenses is easy, sometimes excruciatingly easy. First, write down all of your recurring weekly, monthly, and annual expenses: utility bills, cable and service providers, rent or mortgage, insurance, health care, and so on. Then, get a handle on "petty" expenses: a good exercise is to keep a log of how much money you spend each day for a week. People are often surprised at how those five-dollar lattes, bridge tolls, parking fees, and afternoon snacks add up.

Then, look ahead: create a budget, or projected profit-and-loss statement, for the next twelve months. I find making a row across the top of the page of the next twelve months to be most useful. On the left-hand side of the page, create a column of revenue and expenses. Projecting income can be very difficult to do accurately. An easy place to start is with what your income has been for the past several years; just the facts. Look at your bank statements, and then make your best estimate as to your income for the next twelve months. Then estimate expenses, month by month. A projected budget is particularly revealing and useful and can act as a helpful guide. Put all these financial tools together and you have a good snapshot of your financial picture, now and for the near future. What do you see?

As important, who do you see? What sort of person has this exercise and this portrait revealed? Examine your financial attitudes and habits. Do you spend money too freely or not freely enough? Do you always feel poor or does money come to you and then seem to disappear? Does your impression of how you relate to money actually align with the way you spend or save money? Whatever your money habits are, take stock.

Looking clearly and closely at our financial situation reveals a great deal about our attitudes, habits, and expectations. This can be both satisfying and a relief, when it shines a light on good qualities that may have been hidden, or it can bring up a good deal of avoidance, anxiety, and pain, as we face concrete evidence of our seeming inadequacies, failures, and judgments. It is no wonder that money is named as the most difficult topic for couples to talk about, or that Karen and Thomas (in chapter 4) could look at the same financial data and come to completely opposite conclusions about their financial future. If individuals have such a difficult time openly and skillfully addressing this topic, how much harder to do this with someone else? Many people seem to have creative gaps when it comes to finances. What is enough? Compared to whom? What do you think your income and lifestyle say about who you are? The seemingly straightforward topic of money encompasses many of our deepest assumptions, aspirations, attitudes, and fears. If you feel you don't have enough money, there is suffering and anxiety. And, strangely enough, having too much money can also be experienced as a burden, eliciting suffering and anxiety.

JOY

Conducting a personal audit (as described in chapter 4) should provide you with a snapshot of your daily mood and emotional and physical health. But when we are contemplating a major new goal or life change, we are usually already saying something about how we feel about our current life: what we don't like and what might truly make us joyful. As we've seen, for many of my clients, the impetus for change is a deep dissatisfaction with where they are. Clarify that right now. Make a series of lists or assessments that look separately at four different areas: work, family, community, and spiritual practice.

What do you like and love in your life now? What makes you happy in your work, your relationships, your community, and your spiritual practice? What is in alignment with your needs, desires, hopes, and dreams? Be specific. These lists comprise the things we'd like to keep, whatever change we make.

Then, make separate lists for what's not working. What's missing, bothering you, unfinished, or not showing up at all in your work, your relationships, your community, and your spiritual practice? Just take stock.

One client I worked with created this sort of document and was surprised to find things weren't as distressing as he imagined. You may be closer to your goals than you think in certain areas; sometimes dissatisfactions in one aspect of our lives leads us to forget or ignore what's working well. So, when it comes time below to write the business plan, consider whether changes to fix what isn't working might also negatively impact what is working. This is another reason to approach large goals with small steps — so we can adjust if our strategies are causing more harm than good.

IMPACT

How do you define *impact*? What is meaningful to you? Again, inherent in your vision for what you want will be an expression of the kind of positive impact you want to have. If this wasn't directly stated when you wrote your vision, do so now. Then, take a look at the same four areas above — your work, your family, your community, and your spiritual life — and assess how you are currently doing. What sort of impact do you have in each area? Is there anything missing right now? Be as specific and honest as you can; don't oversell or undersell your influence. As with joy, consider whether you are fully appreciating all the impacts you currently have. Also, be forthright if you notice negative impacts; note them without judgment. Consider both yourself and others: are the impacts always the same or aligned? Consider: Do you hold yourself back from having more impact in your current situation?

Write the F*#%ing Business Plan

Sekito Kisen, an eighth-century Chinese Zen teacher, said, "If you don't know the path right in front of you, how will you know when you are on it?" Sounds to me like this Zen teacher would have been an excellent business coach. I'm surprised by how many individuals and businesses, small and large, don't have a plan. They don't have clear goals and budgets; they lack a set of benchmarks for the next quarter. It seems that when the business is working well, it can be easier to just keep moving ahead. Who needs a plan? And when business is not working well, who has time for planning? The same dynamic seems to hold true for our personal lives (and finances).

Can you recognize when you are on, and when you fall off, the path? Are you simply accepting that whatever effort you make is all you can do? Now, let's write a business plan. At the very least, it is excellent practice for quantifying amorphous qualities like our sense of satisfaction and providing a much-needed reality check. This plan can be applied to a particular project you are working toward, a business endeavor, or another aspect of your life. It is, at heart, a story, just like the hero's journey, and similar steps apply: vision, finances, guides, obstacles, and next steps or actions.

As you develop your plans, regard this as a living document, something to amend and revise as you proceed. In fact, make a point to revisit your business plan periodically, at least twice a year, to see how you're doing, celebrate progress, and adjust expectations.

Vision

By now, you have already articulated your vision. Now, describe it in clear, succinct, concrete terms. Contained within the vision statement should be a description for how you will accomplish it, or what the endpoint looks like. What concrete, measurable results do you hope for? What is the purpose and mission of your project, your business, your life? The vision can be large and audacious or more limited in scope.

For instance, I now work with an organization called Search Inside Yourself Leadership Institute, a nonprofit, educational organization dedicated to training leaders in mindfulness and emotional intelligence. Our vision statement is very simple: Enlightened Leaders Worldwide. Our mission is to bring more happiness and more peace to the world.

Finances

With your balance sheet and profit-and-loss statements completed, you're in position to look ahead and visualize the future in as much detail and openness as possible. Start to put numbers and dates to this vision. One month, six months, and one year from now, what might your expenses and income be as you pursue your goal? Are there benchmarks that you need to meet by certain dates (given how much money or resources you have right now)?

Project what seems likely and fill in the details the best you can. Seek to balance your expectations — not too optimistic, not too conservative. Projecting expenses is generally brutally easier and much more predictable than calculating potential income. Try several possible scenarios, based on likely outcomes; as you define steps and actions below, match them with financial expectations. Make it an exploration, a pleasant and eye-opening exploration.

Then at the end of each month, it is invaluable for you to compare actual results to projections. This is how you learn to make needed adjustments in your thinking and planning and keep moving forward.

Guides and Contacts

Accomplishing any vision involves the help, support, and guidance of others. Identify the people, talents, guides, and connections you will need in order to succeed, and write them by name in your business plan. Specify how and when you will contact each one. What will you ask of them? If you will hire people for certain jobs, specify a budget for them, along with a date when you hope their work will start and finish.

Challenges and Obstacles

By measuring the gap, you have already identified many of the challenges and obstacles you face. List each one in the business plan in direct terms, along with an indication of how you will address it. These challenges can be broken into categories, if it's helpful to think of them that way. The two main categories are external and internal challenges. First, what resources do you need that you don't currently possess, and how will you get them?

This could be money, technology, or finding the right people to work with. If it's a business goal, you may be challenged by competition and the need to identify and get the attention of an audience or customer base.

Then there are the internal challenges. What skills do you need to learn or improve? What habits, attitudes, or self-defeating patterns get in your way? Shed as much light on these as possible. Be honest about these challenges: if you're not a morning person, and your plan calls for you to get up early, how will you address this?

Next Steps and Actions

Finally, all of this thinking and strategizing leads to the heart of the plan itself. What are you going to do? What steps will you take, and when? What are your specific goals, benchmarks, and timelines? Merge all of the thinking you've done so far into a series of clear, concrete steps that describe what you hope to accomplish, and how.

For instance, I had a client whose goal was to start a business. As a general vision statement, it's fine to write, "I plan to create a successful gardening company," but as an action step in a business plan, this is too vague. Instead, phrase action steps in ways that include a time frame, cost, support network, and anticipated outcome. For her plan, my client revised her goal as follows: "I plan to create a freelance gardening and garden consulting company. My goal is to bring in revenue of $7,500 per month by the twelfth month of operations, with net income of $5,000 per month." The client then wrote a detailed marketing plan, a social media strategy, and an operations plan to support her financial projections.

ACCEPT WHAT IS

Your Happiness Index

A coaching client of mine, a successful entrepreneur and scientist, once showed me his happiness assessment. Every day he ranked on a scale from 1 to 10 how he was performing on a variety of areas: work, relationship, spiritual practice, hobbies, exercise, and a few others. He would then calculate an average of these numbers to determine his daily overall happiness quotient. He showed me a chart he kept, tracking the daily rises and falls of this measure. It looked much like the Dow Jones stock market index, with its various trends up and down, seesawing between deep valleys and steep climbs.

I admired his effort to pay attention to and measure his level of happiness. This can be a useful self-awareness tool. He used this tool to determine which parts of his life needed more focus and attention. You, too, could use this approach to provide a quick, daily snapshot.

But I was concerned that he was being aggressively judgmental and hard on himself. His numbers were obviously subjective; after all, he was his own judge, and a harsh one. I suggested that he also keep another version of his happiness index. For this version, I asked that, every day, he rate himself a perfect 10 in every category of his life: work, relationship, spiritual practice, hobbies, exercise. On this second chart no improvement is necessary, or even possible. It represents complete and utter acceptance of one's life right now, in this moment. Complete appreciation, satisfaction with what is.

I hoped, by keeping both charts, he could practice fighting for change and complete acceptance. And that each might help inform the other. Too much driving change, especially when measured solely by judgment and criticism, can lead to a state of constant striving and result in emotional burnout. Too much acceptance can lead to passivity. The goal is not to find a middle spot but to be adept at both — fighting for change and accepting what is.

Just Avoid Picking and Choosing

Zen master Joshu is often regarded as one of the greatest Zen teachers. He lived during the Tang dynasty in ninth-century China. Collections of Zen stories contain many of his colorful, playful, and paradoxical teachings. One story in particular is quite succinct, and famous, and speaks directly to the topic of accepting what is. This story describes how one evening Joshu addressed a large assembly of monks. He said, "The Ultimate Path is without difficulty. Just avoid picking and choosing. As soon as there are words spoken, this is picking and choosing, this is clarity. This old monk does not abide within clarity."

The first lines are very well known in the Zen world, and I quote them often: "The Ultimate Path is without difficulty. Just avoid picking and choosing." This is a caution about judgment. However, I'd forgotten the last two lines of this story, which are rarely quoted and much less well known: "As soon as there are words spoken, this is picking and choosing, this is clarity. This old monk does not abide within clarity."

This brought me up short and even gave me chills. How could I explain anything, much less this teaching, which advises against both words and clarity? Writing this book, I am caught in paradox. The moment we voice our desires, explain our lives, write our business plan, we lose the inexpressible nature of the Ultimate Path. How is this so? More than once, I have found myself surprised by paradox, whose insights are more clear than clear, providing a clarity that is not clarity. I think Joshu might agree with this claim. When we choose one side or the other, it may appear as clear, but something essential is left out.

I had lunch recently with my friend Kaz Tanahashi, a world-renowned calligrapher and translator. He is also one of the most content, happy, and productive people I know. Kaz travels throughout the world teaching calligraphy and leading Zen retreats. He told me that upon returning from his travels recently someone asked him, "What's your favorite city?" What a strange question, he thought. He wondered: If he named a favorite city, then when traveling to a city he hadn't named, would he enjoy this city less? He answered by saying, "There are things I like about all the cities I visit."

Of course, we are assessing, discerning, and "picking and choosing" all the time. We have to. I pick and choose these words. We pick and choose our goals. At the same time, Kaz and Joshu are suggesting that we not fall into a trap when measuring, when we reduce the value of our experiences, and the quality of our lives, by preferring some things and not others, by pitting a favorite against everything that doesn't qualify as a favorite.

I have the same ambivalence with the popular notion of a bucket list — the list of things to do or places to visit before you die. It's a terrific idea for focusing your attention on how to change your life to do the things that really matter to you. But it leaves out acceptance and gratitude. Despite fighting for change, we should recognize that there is nothing lacking from our lives. Our lives are perfect in this moment just as they are. We should be ready to let go, to die today, with open hearts and a sense of profound acceptance and satisfaction.

Buddha described the practice of acceptance this way: If you put a handful of salt into a small bowl of water, the water will be too salty to drink. If you take the same amount of salt and pour it into a river, the water will be drinkable, without any taste of the salt. If your heart is limited, one unkind word or judgment can cause you to suffer. If your heart is large, an unkind word or deed will have little power for you.

What a terrific teaching! Acceptance isn't a technique or something that you can learn by reading a book — not even this book, I'm afraid. It is essentially opening your heart, living with an open heart, working with an open heart. And this is not easy because we are always so profoundly picking and choosing, limiting and judging ourselves and others, our experience, our life. Your life is meaningful to you no matter what you do. How can you pick and choose, then let go of picking and choosing and treasure each moment?

Nothing Lacking: A Practice

Imagine, just for these next few minutes, that there is absolutely nothing lacking from your life right now. Begin with your list of projects. Imagine that you've either completed them or let them go. For whatever reason, your list of projects is empty, complete. No more articles or books to write. No more languages to learn, skills to improve. The way you dance now, fine; your current cooking skills, also fine.

Whatever self-help plan this chapter has led you to develop, imagine it is complete. Nothing left to do. Add to this your plans for others — children, parents, partner, friends. All the people you want to change, for the better — this list is complete or empty. Everyone in your life is providing everything you want from them. Picture nothing left to add, change, or improve.

Now, just for this moment, notice whatever you are feeling, touching, hearing, seeing, tasting. Let your senses come alive.

See if you can be curious without picking and choosing. How does it feel? Who are you without your judgments? Just notice this person, without trying to do anything extra.

The Laziness Expert

I was recently interviewed by a major national magazine for a story they were writing about laziness. Since I'm the author of a book called *Less*, they apparently thought I'd be a good spokesperson.

I initially resisted the label of laziness and attempted to reframe the discussion, talking not about laziness but about mindfulness. I began the interview by quoting Brother David Steindl-Rast: "The antidote to exhaustion isn't rest; the antidote to exhaustion is wholeheartedness." I then launched into the topic of meaning and mindfulness, of acceptance and how doing less is not being lazy.

The young woman interviewing me interrupted and said, "You don't understand. This article is about laziness. Our readers, soccer moms and middle-aged women, are burned-out and exhausted. We want them to know that being lazy is a good thing."

I needed to think quickly on my feet. To give the writer what she wanted, I needed to change my usual view of myself and the world. Could I accept, openly and honestly, this new framework that was being presented to me? Could I promote laziness?

"Well, my wife and I just took the month of September off and traveled around Europe. And when I cook in the kitchen, I'm always trying to do the most with the least amount of effort. And I take a nap in the middle of the day, almost every day. How's that for laziness?"

"That's what I'm looking for!" the interviewer said.

I kept going and really got into it: when I'm organizing my schedule, I try to drive as little as possible; recently at the farmer's market, I've been buying a number of prepared and frozen food items that don't require cooking. I go for a walk nearly every day. I love relaxing, playing, looking for ways to get the most done with the least amount of effort. When the interview was finished, the interviewer thanked me profusely. She had much more material than she needed.

It was an eye-opening experience. Among the CEOs and executives in my coaching practice, *lazy* is a four-letter word. And I don't usually think of the things I mentioned as laziness, but if framing it in this way is helpful, I'll gladly become a proponent of laziness.

Now, as a recognized expert on the topic, I highly recommend laziness. Is it bad? Only if that's what you pick and choose. Many of my coaching clients also see *acceptance* as a dirty word, as a euphemism for "giving up" or "not trying." Certainly, acceptance has a potentially negative side. At what point does acceptance become passivity; when does taking naps and going for walks become goofing off? I won't say! But if laziness is what some people call taking care of ourselves in the midst of demanding and often overbusy lives, I'm all for it.

No need to feel guilty. Relax. Practice pausing. Go for long walks. Read poetry in the middle of the day. Take a weekly Sabbath. Take that much-needed break or vacation. Take time each day to just appreciate being alive. These are all valuable practices that can help lead to wholeheartedness. Indeed, go back and insert these things into your business plan. Perhaps, by taking time to accept your life just as it is, you might find yourself better prepared and energized to fight for important changes.

Constantly Lower Your Standards

Don't keep searching for the truth;
Just let go of your opinions.

— SENG TS'AN, *THE MIND OF ABSOLUTE TRUST*

After nearly thirty years of marriage, one filled with the usual and unusual ups and downs of any long-term relationship, my wife and I decided to have a recommitment ceremony in our home. We invited a small group of close friends, people who had known us for many years. Most had been our friends since before our marriage, and most had themselves been in long-term marriages. During the ceremony that we designed, we asked each person in attendance to speak to the central issue of the ceremony: What is the secret of long-term relationships? There were many wise and useful responses. I was sorry that we didn't record them all.

To me, the most memorable response was from a woman who had been married to her husband for over thirty years. They were both very accomplished people, with two very successful grown children. The wife looked at her husband and said, "The secret to long-term relationships is to constantly lower your standards." Of course, everyone laughed. Then she went on to say that the secret of long-term relationships is to realize that love includes hatred and pain and difficulty, as well as joy and happiness and serenity.

But I felt a deeper layer of helpfulness to what she said. The way I heard her answer is that the secret of long-term relationships is just to love — just love without comparing, without criticizing, without measuring. Accept yourself and your partner with an open and loving heart. Love and see what happens without expectations.

Or, to put her offering another way: How do you avoid the

seemingly inevitable accumulation of disappointments that can eat away at loving relationships over time? Constantly lowering your standards, in this context, means to forget standards: yours and even your spouse's. It means, strange as it sounds, to forget the constant and calculated measurements of who you are and who your partner is and what you need in terms of that person. These standards are almost always one-sided and to varying degrees inaccurate. Our expectations of the other person not only are unhelpful but can be truly harmful to a marriage or long-term relationship. What happens as soon as we compare our partner to our standards and find him or her wanting? We imply, and may come to believe, that there must be someone better out there, a marriage or relationship that is more perfect, a type of union more satisfying than the one we have. Reality is not good enough.

I've noticed that this dynamic applies within any relationship, including our relationship with ourselves, which is the longest-term relationship we have. Our list of disappointments with others sometimes doesn't hold a candle to the list we create for ourselves. In my leadership development practice, in working with teams, and in all the relationships that I have been part of, I've seen that whenever people go down the road of identifying right and wrong, of who did (or did not do) what to whom, of who is or isn't measuring up to a preconceived image, it almost always leads to the same place. Someone, or everyone, feels hurt, and trust, intimacy, and understanding suffer. People shut down and become even less effective. In order for us to grow, to feel alive, it is valuable to aim high and work hard to bridge our creative gaps, and accept the results with gratitude. Set high standards, then forget about your standards. Open your heart. Fight for change. Accept what is.

Chapter 7

EMBRACE EMOTION, EMBODY EQUANIMITY

There is a crack in everything.
That's how the light gets in.

— Leonard Cohen

I was recently at a business conference of more than four hundred social entrepreneurs, nonprofit leaders, and CEOs of successful companies that had some form of social mission. Success and opportunity, joy and celebration were in abundance. After a session on how to raise more capital for your growing business, I was approached by Todd, the CEO of a fairly large and apparently successful media company. Todd and I had talked over many years while attending these conferences, but I did not know him well. He pulled me aside and said that, though we barely knew each other, he trusted me and thought I might be able to offer some assistance. We found an empty room just off the main hallway and sat down, and he began to describe his current situation.

Since the 2008 economic recession, his business had been facing significant challenges. He had lost some key customers, and
his revenue was nearly 10 percent below the previous year's. He
was feeling anxious and was not sleeping well. He was having
trouble focusing. He found himself irritable and at times reacting angrily with employees. A few key employees had recently
resigned, and he was feeling like the captain on the helm of a
sinking ship — a large, beautiful ship that he had built over the
past fifteen years. His tension and anxiety were also affecting his
marriage and his relationships with his children. He felt lost. His
business and his life seemed to be unraveling.

I told him I appreciated his openness. How strange to know
someone for so many years and never really deeply connect. I
also thought I knew what he was going through. It reminded me
of some of the times when I was CEO of Brush Dance. At times, I
faced significant challenges and didn't know if the business would
survive. This hurt in very personal ways: I felt keenly how much
of my own sense of identity was connected to my work and the
company's success. In these moments, the fear of loss, the fear
of embarrassment, and the fear of letting others down seemed to
drive every decision.

In that moment, I also wondered: How much pain and difficulty was residing beneath the surface for the attendees of this
conference? I had developed many close personal relationships
with a good number of people there, and I was aware of situations and challenges from many people's personal lives: difficult
family relationships, recent deaths, divorces, cancers and other
illnesses, and significant personal losses. Almost no one, though,
admitted what Todd shared with me: stories of business and job
failures and the significant personal challenges that resulted, like
sleeplessness, depression, and anxiety.

I asked Todd if he was interested in exploring a mindfulness and meditation practice. He was enthusiastic, so we started right then and there. We spent a few minutes doing a short guided meditation; pausing, bringing attention to our breath, body, and feelings. Just noticing whatever was there, including the pain and fears. Checking in with our thinking as well as our heart. He expressed his interest in continuing to develop these practices. He recognized that he needed to slow down the busyness of his mind, find more ease and confidence within himself, and change the way he was both creating and responding to stressful situations. I directed him to some websites as well as phone applications that could support him in the continuation of a mindfulness practice.

Then we spoke about steps he might take to build a support system — being part of a group, renewing his relationship with a therapist, taking yoga classes. And we addressed business changes — hiring talented employees, taking a fresh look at his products, rebuilding relationships with existing customers, and reviewing and revisiting his plans to either expand revenue or reduce costs.

Todd's dilemma is a common one in the business world and the world of work, and it's one that's rarely acknowledged or discussed. We each care tremendously about our work lives: the businesses or organizations we are part of or create, the products and services we offer, the problems we solve, the coworkers and employees we nurture, and our personal accomplishments on the job. For many people, this basic need to care, to have your heart and mind fully engaged in a meaningful endeavor, has been squelched — by working in large impersonal organizations or in smaller organizations that don't honor or recognize the importance of caring, of bringing your full self to work. The solution is not to care less, but to care more, while learning to manage our caring. Caring without equanimity can hurt our effectiveness and lead to personal despair. Not caring enough, or at all, also hurts our effectiveness and can lead to cynicism and despair. Finding the proper balance, and maintaining our balance, between emotions and equanimity is perhaps the most difficult of the five paradoxes. It's the one I see people struggle with the most, whatever the context. More often than not, when we fall off the tightrope, it's our emotions that push us.

EMBRACE EMOTION, EMBODY EQUANIMITY ACTION PLAN

How do we meet the challenge in every moment of finding, embodying, and expressing the most effective response? We begin by learning and following the practices in this chapter.

1. Look at your life through the lens of the eight imprisonments (page 184): Simply consider or meditate on them, or use each as a journal-writing prompt.
2. Embrace difficult emotions through the practice of feeling miserable (page 191).
3. Embrace joyful emotions by noticing the good in everyday life (page 192).
4. Practice cultivating equanimity (page 197) through the following actions:
    Gratefulness (page 198)
    Kindness (page 199)
    Compassion (page 200)
    Sympathetic joy (page 200)
    Taking responsibility (page 201)

EMBRACE EMOTION

The Business World's Dirty Little Secret: We're all human. We all have feelings.

That's the dirty little secret of the business world, the wrench in the gears of progress. People, mucking up the works with their anger, joy, fear, frustration, love, and excitement. Often, that's our dirty little secret, too. We want to be efficient and effective, productive and competent, and feelings are almost always messy and disruptive, or unexpected and unfathomable. We'd usually prefer our lives to be structured, orderly, unfolding with clock-work certainty. We know we possess feelings; they get hurt all the time. But particularly when it comes to our jobs, we think we should be above them. We should be able to avoid them, or ignore them, or control them when we want to, when they get in our way and cause problems.

Yet whether we see emotions as good or bad, positive or neg-ative, we can't escape them. We care. We desire and fear, and we love, and we have to deal with these reactions. The first step is recognizing that emotions are both inevitable and temporary.

They pass and they return. Emotions are only a "problem" when we are unskillful in working with them or when we attempt to avoid them or pretend they don't exist.

Not so long ago, the old assembly-line model dominated the organization of many US businesses and influenced society, and it still has great appeal. It continues to influence today's corporate culture more than you might think. In this model, most employees are trained to do one specific job, while only a few manage or understand the larger process. People then function much like machinery, as easily replaceable cogs performing a single simple task in the great wheel of industry. On an assembly line, each person does his or her part, with no thinking or emotions necessary, and no collaboration. When the assembly line was first developed in the early part of the twentieth century, it proved to be an extremely efficient method for building complicated products, like cars, and it was soon widely emulated throughout industry and business.

But a funny thing happened. Requiring workers to leave the most essential aspects of their lives at the factory door — their emotions and their intelligence, their caring and concern — created its own debilitating inefficiencies. The most famous example in today's organizational effectiveness lore is the story of General Motors. For decades at GM, the unwritten law was "Don't stop the line." Management believed that keeping the car assembly line going at all times was essential. Clearly, stopping the line, for any reason, meant cars and trucks were not being assembled. But as much as that, according to a thirty-year GM employee, management assumed that "if the line stopped, workers would play cards or goof off." GM didn't trust that its own workers cared, and they treated them that way, as unthinking, unfeeling parts that would go idle the moment the line switched off.

As a result of this philosophy and way of working, problems were ignored instead of being addressed. Defective cars, those with missing parts or parts put in backward, rolled off the line and were put into their own special "defective" lot, to await fixing. This lot grew to enormous proportions. At some point, addressing and fixing these problem cars became too costly, and they were essentially abandoned.

In 2008, during the nation's economic downturn, General Motors went into bankruptcy and was bailed out by the federal government (and the American taxpayers). There were many reasons for the company's downfall, and many different problems, but one significant issue was GM's reputation for producing poor-quality vehicles. One major reason for this was GM's "Don't stop the line" attitude, which was embedded in the company's planning and strategy as well as its assembly line. Don't stop to fix problems; just keep doing what you are doing and everything will be fine.

As part of its federal bailout and restructuring in 2008, General Motors entered into a collaboration with Toyota called NUMMI (New United Motor Manufacturing, Inc.). As part of this, GM assembly workers were sent to a Toyota factory in Fremont, California, while several GM managers were flown to Japan to learn the Japanese methodology for building cars. What they discovered was an amazing *aha!* moment. At Toyota, anyone on the assembly line who has a concern about the quality of a part can stop the line at any time. Problems are addressed immediately, with groups of workers getting together to figure out how to solve them. Toyota managers assume that their workers want to build the best cars possible. Constant improvement is the company motto, and this attitude is integrated into all aspects of car production. Workers might have one job, but they are encouraged to think of the entire process. Teams are assembled to discuss problems, look for insights, and develop better methods for producing problem-free cars. In this way, Toyota has been able to consistently build better-quality cars with greater efficiency and lower costs than its American counterparts.

It is easy to look at GM and see their folly. But are we so different? In my coaching and consulting practice, I notice many versions of "Don't stop the line." In some companies, it takes the form of "Don't question the boss" or "Don't confront the rude star salesperson." For my clients, it can translate as "Don't acknowledge anger or fear" or "Don't question the plan or path or career I've committed myself to." A problem crops up, and rather than deal with it, or think strategically and critically about how to redesign our situation to eliminate it, we simply shove it aside and keep working. We become unhappy and don't see this as reason enough to stop the line. Indeed, in many subtle and not-so-subtle ways we are told, especially at work, that our personal happiness and satisfaction are unimportant so long as we do our job. Our daily lives and even our most important relationships can become like assembly lines, in which we move from task to task without allowing ourselves time to stop, admit mistakes or dissatisfactions, and work collaboratively with others to change in ways that are good for everyone.

Instead, our focus, at all costs, is to just get stuff done. It takes courage to stop, acknowledge breakdowns, and ask difficult questions. Thankfully, the business world today has started to recognize the need for this. Making our lives and our companies successful requires listening, flexibility, vision, passion, collaboration, and teamwork — that is, people skills and emotional competencies. Increasingly, companies and organizations are beginning to discover this secret. People who care, people who are emotionally developed and aligned, not only are a competitive advantage but may perhaps be *the* competitive advantage of any organization.

Numerous studies have demonstrated that working skillfully with emotions leads to greater productivity and stronger leadership as well as a greater sense of well-being. One study listed the top six skills that distinguish star performers from average performers in technology companies. These are as follows:

1. Strong achievement drive
2. Ability to influence
3. Conceptual thinking
4. Analytical ability
5. Initiative
6. Self-confidence

Of the top six, only two (conceptual thinking and analytical ability) are intellectual competencies. The other four, including the top two, are emotional competencies. Clearly, even in technology companies, emotional skills lead to better performance at work.

Emotional well-being has also been connected to profits in business. The cover of the January–February 2012 *Harvard Business Review* featured a large, round yellow smiley face with dollar signs at the corners of its smile and the headline "The Value of Happiness: How Employee Well-Being Drives Profits." The world of business, perhaps for the first time since the invention of the factory, is acknowledging the importance of emotions and the relationship between emotions and effectiveness, vision and caring, happiness and profits. Business leaders, management, and owners are exploring how to skillfully negotiate this terrain. And if it can work in the no-nonsense, put-up-or-shut-up world of business, then it certainly is important for each of us as individuals in the heart of our own lives. This is where we develop the emotional competencies that business is learning to want and value. It constitutes a critical personal and spiritual journey of transformation, in which we embrace the very emotions that we struggle with in order to embody the equanimity that makes us effective, so we can quickly regain our balance even when difficult problems arise.

One Key, Eight Prisons

Why are emotions so challenging? Why is there so much emotional despair in our lives, both at work and outside of it? What are some of the unacknowledged dilemmas? Chögyam Trungpa — an important modern Tibetan Buddhist teacher who died in 1987 — spoke of a set of eight states of being that describe dilemmas we all face. He called these experiences the Eight Imprisonments. He called them imprisonments because they are stories, powerful and compelling stories, that limit us and narrow our possibilities. They prevent us from relaxing and opening to just being present, just being happy, and thus they keep us from being effective in our day-to-day lives. Paradoxically, the only way to escape these prisons is to accept that we reside within them. We must embrace our emotions in order to find the freedom to choose how we respond. This is another way we live the insight that we must both know ourselves and forget ourselves. Here are the eight states of being:

Pleasure and pain
Gain and loss
Fame and disgrace
Praise and blame

Pleasure and Pain

We all want pleasure and we don't want pain. Yet by seeking pleasure and avoiding pain we blind ourselves to deeper and more important activities, priorities, and states of mind. Wanting pleasure and avoiding pain is often a state of fear; we're responding to an anxiety born of our imagination. We reach for certain things and avoid other types of things because we anticipate a certain result. This is a very different state of mind than just being present, being aware, and meeting whatever arises in our lives.

Of course, physical pain is a message from our body that something is hurting us; when we feel it, we know we must do something for self-protection, like pull our hand out of a fire. We might think that emotional pain is different, but the brain does not make a distinction between them. Thus, most pain is first registered and experienced in the same way, no matter the cause, and it's up to us to develop the presence of mind to distinguish causes and act appropriately. David Rock, in his book *Your Brain at Work*, beautifully describes and unpacks this dynamic. His focus is the workplace, but his model applies to any human group. His work in neuroscience has uncovered that when we perceive a loss or emotional injury in any of five areas — what he calls SCARF, or status, certainty, autonomy, relatedness, and fairness — this registers as pain in the brain, just the same as a stubbed toe does. Think about your own work situation and the people you work with. Is it painful, and do people react in pain, when there is a loss of status, whether in title, money, or power; when uncertainty arises that threatens one's sense of stability and safety; when a person's autonomy is reduced or taken away, and he or she no longer has decision-making power; when there is a lack of trust and empathy that impairs relatedness; or when fairness is compromised? When any of these threats becomes too great, we withdraw, becoming defensive, and collaboration becomes nearly impossible.

The encouraging news is that our brains and our emotions have a high level of flexibility, or plasticity. We can change how we perceive pleasure and pain and how we respond. As we also know, the same event can sometimes be experienced as either, or both, depending on our perspective in the moment. A scary movie, a good workout, meeting a challenge, love: so many things invoke an inseparable mix of pleasure and pain. By valuing only one and avoiding the other, we miss the essence and lose what we seek. Yet by adjusting our perspective, we can change the game entirely. Through insight and practice, we can embrace experience in its entirety and not be caught up in attempting to manage our experience in a self-protective yet self-defeating way.

Gain and Loss

It is easy to become attached to, even obsessed with, gain. More, more, more is our cultural anthem. More money, more information, more sex, more stuff. In business we've defined corporate responsibility as "maximizing shareholder wealth." Conversely, we will do anything, at almost any cost, to avoid loss — loss of money, of property, of toys, of status and reputation. Certainly, our culture is obsessed with avoiding the loss of our youth and appearance.

Seeking gain and avoiding loss can at times completely undermine our priorities and sensibilities. Even when we know better, the urge can be impossible to resist. Remember the dot-com bubble in the late 1990s? At first, it wasn't seen as a bubble. It was a thrilling new economy that magically showered riches on anyone with a website or online enterprise. Who wouldn't want to be part of such possibility? I jumped in. As CEO of Brush Dance, I created BrushDance.com. For about a year, I became wealthy — on paper. The projected value of the company skyrocketed. Then the bubble burst, and I was left shaken by the emotional pain of loss and failure. Within a span of months the company's value plummeted, my identity and reputation felt damaged, and the company suffered from the upheaval. Looking back, I'm less surprised that I got involved (since few of us can escape the lure of more) than in how I let my own sense of self become attached to the outcome. It was not healthy or accurate. One day we have more, and one day we have less, and that's the way of the world.

Fame and Disgrace

Fame and disgrace are not just the territory of movie stars, television personalities, and celebrity athletes. In subtle and not-so-subtle ways, it's difficult to avoid seeking fame and avoiding disgrace in whatever world we inhabit. If only — if only we were recognized for our innovative ideas, our sense of humor, our kind heart, our wonderful accomplishments. (If only we would recognize this in ourselves.) We want to be admired; we want to embody a certain persona or particular good qualities. If only others would see us. Maybe this job, this activity, this relationship will be the one. The flip side is the fall from grace: the fear that we will make a mistake, or be found wanting, and be seen as the opposite of what we desire.

Fame and disgrace are powerful motivators. Pursuing one and fleeing the other provides us with lots of energy and movement. Of course, we all want to be known as skillful and competent in what we do. We want a good reputation: to be known as responsible, honest, a person of integrity. These are positive desires. The real issue is this: reputation is the result of one's actions, and it's ephemeral. It comes, goes, and changes, and we cannot always control it. We are only being self-serving when we pursue fame for its own sake, when it's the rationale for our actions. Then we are trying to fill an emotional need that resides within, and this is what becomes blinding and debilitating.

Indeed, fame looks very attractive until you achieve it. I have worked with several clients who would be considered famous within their spheres of influence. I've seen firsthand that fame does not solve our problems. Not only do we still have all the same problems and challenges we had before, but now we have new ones. Like endless wealth and ultimate pleasure, fame's glittering illusion is of some permanent status free from toil, doubt, and pain. And yet striving for this or clinging to it does not make it so.

Praise and Blame

When things go right, we'd like to hope we've played a part in making them right, and we'd all like to be recognized for our efforts. We'd all like positive recognition for the good things we've done, for our good intentions, for just being who we are. Conversely, when things go wrong, we'd like to hope we haven't contributed to the error. If we have, we'd also like to hope that we will willingly accept our portion of responsibility. But only our portion. If others are involved, we want them named, too. And if those others are more responsible than we are, then we may insist they shoulder most of the blame (and suffer most of the consequences). Blame is hard to accept, and we are quick to parse facts and impressions so that blame gets spread around or even shifted entirely onto someone else.

As with all the eight dilemmas, praise and blame are problematic mostly to the degree that we cling to or avoid them. And like all the dilemmas, how we experience them usually rests on judgment. We pick and choose: good or bad, right or wrong, pleasure or pain. Despite our best intentions, we can almost never be certain of all the consequences of our actions. Have you ever had the experience of receiving praise and blame for the same action? Every person has a different point of view, and each can be true (or reflect an authentic, honest response). So, we must learn to accept praise and blame equally, and let them go equally, seeing them as passing judgments of limited perspective and usefulness.

Praise, in the business world, is often treated like an unalloyed positive action. It's a grease gun for the office's sticky wheels. I myself often coach executives to unleash recognition and to acknowledge more freely the people around them. My clients will be more effective and create a more effective workforce if they don't take anyone's efforts for granted. This acknowledgment, though, must be real and authentic. If we give false praise only to make someone feel better, or only to make ourselves look good in his or her eyes, then it will backfire. Giving and receiving recognition becomes cheapened; it becomes a cover or substitute for real trust, empathy, and connection. Blame can also be a cover, a way to prevent having important, difficult conversations about shared responsibilities, impacts, and expectations. We may feel justified blaming someone for a problem, but by doing so, have we solved anything? Or have we just kept the assembly line moving?

Resistance Is Futile

A very earnest Zen student asks his teacher, "How can I avoid the discomfort of hot and cold?"

The teacher responds, "Go to that place where there is no hot and no cold."

"Where is that place?" the student asks.

"When you are hot, be hot, and when you are cold, be cold," the teacher responds.

Ah, another cryptic Zen story! This story is also quite famous and was handed down from a collection of stories from eighth-century China. The story addresses the seesaw of our emotions:

they swing between extremes, and not always in ways we enjoy. So what do we do? The message is simple: Be present. Show up. Be here now! When you are happy, just be fully happy. When irritated or angry, be irritated or angry. When at work, be at work. When at play, fully play. As Harry Roberts would say with a laugh, real simple.

The trouble is, we so rarely allow ourselves to be fully present, to fully accept the present moment. In practice, this isn't easy at all. In our modern lives, we have become so split and so distracted that we are not even aware of the splits and distractions. When it is hot, we go racing for the air-conditioning. When it is cold, we go racing for the heater. When we are happy, we worry that it won't last. When we are sad, grieving, and miserable, we seek any kind of relief or distraction. But if we would escape discomfort and suffering, then we must not resist the present moment, whatever it is. Accept it. If you are grieving, weep until the tears are gone. Be hot, be cold, and know this moment will pass.

The story's message is to shift our perspective and actions; don't try to micromanage the world. Stay with what is. Appreciate the beautiful sunsets and the pains of failure and loss, and trust that from this place real change emerges that leads to freedom and equanimity. Don't spend your energy fighting against your experience. This is a trap.

For instance, when my colleague Todd approached me at the conference, he was in a good deal of pain. He didn't want to be in pain, and he reached out and asked for my help. Yet the first thing I did was ask him if he wanted to start a mindfulness practice, and in this way fully feel and enter his pain. He did, and the effects were immediate: the experience of pain bloomed and then subsided. Much of the trouble Todd was finding himself in was from trying to avoid his emotions. He was unsuccessfully bottling up his fear, hurt, and anger, and he was lashing out at his employees. As a result, he had lost some of his most talented people. Over time, Todd has continued to face and accept his business situation, and to work with his own emotional life, and he has been making significant progress in putting his business and personal life back together.

Embrace Difficulty

Most people don't like any form of discomfort and attempt to avoid pain and difficulty at all costs. We don't like to grieve, but grief is a beautiful and natural response to important losses. This practice of embracing difficulty and loss is primarily about noticing, just paying attention and being present and alive for our lives. Any and all difficult situations — whether large or small, whether petty irritations and embarrassments or coping with the death of loved ones — can bring up unresolved feelings, old habits, and patterns that stir up unpleasant emotions and self-criticism. As a practice, embracing difficulty and loss is a way to turn the situation upside down, or at least to look at ourselves and our responses from a different perspective. We accept the difficulties and losses that come our way so that we might learn from them, so that we might use them in a positive way to be better, stronger, more adept. We examine our resistance, fear, and denial so that we might know ourselves better, accept ourselves better, question better, and increase our self-confidence. In this way, we create more possibility for openness and appreciation even in the midst of resentment, jealousy, and sorrow.

One practice that I often suggest to coaching clients (and use myself) is what I call the practice of feeling miserable. This isn't for everyone, but I've noticed that many people have well-honed and time-tested strategies for avoiding difficult emotions and for not feeling bad. At times we find ourselves in impossibly difficult situations. Sometimes we just feel lousy or downright miserable. As I like to say, being a human being is a tough gig. And there are times when, for whatever reason, we just feel pain. Allowing ourselves to fully feel that pain can be a way to open, to expand our hearts. We can feel our deep connection with our families and wider communities, and surprisingly, open the gates to deeper feelings of joy. Allowing ourselves to feel miserable can also be an effective way to not avoid the truth of the present moment; we drop our defenses, stop trying to shelter ourselves, and deal directly and effectively with what is. In a work context, dropping down into our feelings can be the first step toward taking effective action.

I generally do this practice, and recommend doing this practice, during a morning meditation period — just taking a few minutes to check in with myself, noticing any feelings of sadness, grief, and longing in my heart. Just letting myself touch this pain, without bracing or holding back. Then, letting go of these thoughts and feelings, I bring my attention back to the breath and body. Sometimes I use this time to send wishes of well-being, happiness, and peace to my family and friends, to the world, and to myself. This combination of feeling and acknowledging pain and stating my intention to bring peace into the world helps me to settle and opens my heart.

Embrace Joy

A large part of developing equanimity, which I discuss just below, is developing the practice of embracing joy. However, embracing joy is also a companion to the practice of embracing difficulty. During challenging situations we sometimes can miss the joy, the little surprising things that happen sometimes right in the midst of frustration. See both, in whatever measure they exist.

I think back to the time when my daughter was in third grade. I drove her to school most mornings, down the hill to Tam Valley School, about a five-minute drive. Often the mood during the drive was one of quiet satisfaction, after the morning whirlwind of waking her up, a few minutes of reading to her in bed, getting up, getting dressed, eating breakfast, packing for school, and hustling out the door in time to be at school before 7:45 AM. Some mornings the whirlwind was stressful and frustrating. The shout "I can't find my socks!" blaring from the living room while I was cooking breakfast and packing lunches was enough to crumple this Zen teacher's composure, giving rise to such thoughts as "I had children, why?" and "Where is the nearest exit?" One of our family myths that survives to this day is the time that I became so frustrated helping my daughter locate her socks that when I found one I threw it at her in anger. Clearly, this story is made up. Or perhaps I was merely throwing the socks to her with a bit too much enthusiasm. In truth, I totally lost it. I was completely triggered. This scene had "amygdala hijack" written all over it (the amygdala being an emotional center of the brain, which constantly scans for threats and rewards). I also recall times at the kitchen table with our eight-year-old daughter and eleven-year-old son, having to gently, and at times not so gently, remind them that breakfast was a noncontact sport.

While I remember the frustrations, these have faded compared to the joys, which were woven in and around the difficult moments, side by side. Hot popovers coming out of the oven actually popped, causing smiling faces and cheers of success. Laughter, giggling, and play. Surprising questions and conversations about boys, about girls, about kissing; about life, death, and music. Some mornings just looking at their faces, two beautiful beings, made my heart sing or melt. Many days this joy was tempered, and other times heightened, by the knowledge that they would grow up, and I would not be needed to wake them up, make them breakfast, drive them to school. Today, even the moments of frustration are tinged with longing.

One morning conversation on the way to third grade with my daughter stands out. I asked her if she could remember a time that made her particularly happy. She thought about this but also seemed somewhat perplexed by the question. Then she turned and looked at me and said, "Daddy, I laugh all day long."

EMBODY EQUANIMITY

Patience in the Hell Realm

In the book *The Art of Happiness at Work* by the Dalai Lama and Howard Cutler, Cutler tells the story of interviewing His Holiness. Cutler was describing the challenges and difficult situations many people face at work — too much to do and not enough time, lack of fairness, dehumanizing work environments — and at one point in the conversation the Dalai Lama laughed and said, "Your questions are impossible! It is almost as if you are asking, 'How can beings in the hell realm learn to practice patience, tolerance, and tranquility?'"

Well, in fact, that is exactly what we want (as the Dalai Lama well knows). It is easy to feel good and practice equanimity when troubles are small. But when our life starts to look and feel like hell — when we fall off the tightrope and getting back on seems impossible — that's when we need help, desperately. Does this situation sound familiar: too much to do, not enough time, and a lack of fairness at work (or in the world)? Sadly, these have become the norm in our culture. Perhaps you scoff at the idea of a dehumanizing work environment: for most of us, the demeaning, restrictive, even cruel working conditions of prior generations no longer exist. However, I also think many people have given up and now accept a debilitating and unfulfilling status quo: sitting in stale cubicles and doing "assembly-line" jobs in workplaces that lack collaboration, honest and open communication, and cultivation of our intellect and creativity. We no longer recognize what we have given up, what we truly want. Many of us no longer see the possibility of supportive, kind, joyful, and even loving work environments.

The word *equanimity* comes from Latin roots for *even* and *mind*. Whatever enters your mind you meet with spaciousness while maintaining, or quickly regaining, your balance. The practice of equanimity is the practice of acceptance without indifference. It is practicing deep caring and love without clinging or attachment. It is the method for negotiating the third truth: accepting what is while fighting for change. As a practice, it's a way of stepping back to look at our lives and our world as though from a distance so as to see the truth of our situation, and yet to remain emotionally aware, connected, and alive. It is sometimes described as looking over a mountain range with a sense of connection and awe or as looking over all of humanity without discrimination.

Equanimity is a practice that may sound either strange or unattainable to our twenty-first-century ears but is neither. Equanimity is based on the experience that everything changes. Whatever we see or experience is temporary. Equanimity is the antidote to the anxiety and restlessness this realization may cause. Equanimity laughs in the face of security, instead realizing and finding comfort and steadiness in the midst of insecurity. This may sound daunting and impossible, but we do it all the time. Indeed, I call having equanimity a practice because it is an action; it is something we must do, not just a philosophical idea to ponder. One everyday example is found in driving our cars: we zip along at death-defying speeds, simultaneously alert to the myriad and swiftly changing dangers while singing along happily to the radio. Driving safely and effectively means developing equanimity behind the wheel: being neither frozen by fear nor blithely unaware. Now, how might we achieve this in the rest of our life, to make us more effective, calmer, happier?

In Buddhist psychology equanimity is the seventh in what are known as the seven factors of awakening. One of the compelling aspects of Buddhist teaching is the understanding that within each person are the seeds of complete freedom and awareness. We just need to practice, to put our attention to these abilities, to "wake up" to what is — the actuality that each moment, each experience, is fresh and alive. How interesting that equanimity is considered the ultimate or seventh of these practices. The first six are mindfulness, or the practice of attention and present-moment awareness; curiosity, or the practice of questioning and investigating; energy, which is the practice of being proactive and moving through difficulty; joy, the practice of resting in the happiness of appreciating being alive; ease, which is knowing how to rest even in the midst of activity; and concentration, or the ability to focus fully on what you are doing. These seven practices or qualities are sometimes described as limbs on a tree, and we are the tree.

With equanimity, you can see and embrace emotions and respond to them without being caught up in them or giving in to despair or indifference. You could think of equanimity like the "pause" between feeling and acting that allows us to choose what seeds to water. It is cultivating the ability to choose well, with patience and compassion, even when we find ourselves in the hell realm.

Practices for Cultivating Equanimity

It takes practice to cultivate and awaken joy and kindness. Equanimity doesn't come easily; it is much easier to describe than to do. Yet it can be approached just like any other "creative gap": it's possible to identify where you are now, to measure the distance to where you want to be, and then to take practical actions to get there. Just setting your intention to try is the biggest step. This brings awareness and focus, and awareness is the key.

For instance, we all find that it's easier to be compassionate, kind, patient, and nonjudgmental in certain circumstances, and with some people, than others. That's natural. This is another reason we must work to know ourselves well, so we can learn to recognize and transform our ineffective and self-defeating reactions. Equanimity is a skill we need when things are most difficult, and we learn it by practicing on our most difficult emotions. So, the first step in practicing equanimity is to embrace our emotions, accept difficulty, and recognize what's true. Once we can do that, we can transform our difficulties by putting into practice the specific actions below. While these actions are beneficial at any time, and with or without any specific reason to do them, they become powerful, transformative lessons in equanimity when they are practiced in specific reaction to the eight dilemmas and the many destructive emotions they inspire: attachment, fear, anger, greed, frustration, and so on.

In order to bring more consciousness and self-awareness to this work, consider practicing one of the actions below for a week and tracking your experience in a journal. At the end of each day, for twenty minutes, conduct an "audit" of the day: when did the issue come up, how did you react, and what were the circumstances? Notice if there are patterns to what triggers you or to certain reactions. Just notice, and in this way keep encouraging self-awareness in your most difficult situations.

Gratefulness

Of all the practices, gratefulness may be the most powerful, and it's one of the easiest to practice on the run. If you can make gratefulness a habit, many other good qualities follow.

First, begin and end each day by expressing gratitude, and be specific. Name what you are grateful for: life itself, a roof over your head, clean water and air, a job and income, family and friends, the fragrance of a flower, a funny cartoon. Right now, in this particular moment, what are you grateful for?

Spread the practice of gratefulness throughout your day. Consider keeping an ongoing gratefulness journal: write down things you are grateful for as you think of them, and keep this in your pocket and on your desk. Refer to it; open it at random whenever you notice it. Isn't this why we keep photographs of our family and loved ones in our offices? To remember to be grateful for them? If your work space lacks such reminders, add some. Include photographs of meaningful places, anything that has meaning for you that helps to wake you up and remind you of what you appreciate.

Throughout your day, practice being consciously grateful for small compliments, acts of kindness, and other positive actions. In this way, we can "balance" our natural focus on problems, bad news, and negative events, especially at work. Emergencies, mistakes, and accidents need our focused attention and effective action, but they don't need to overwhelm our inner experience.

Indeed, whenever you find yourself resentful, depressed, and grumbling that life is unfair, practice expressing gratitude, even including for the problem and painful emotions themselves. After all, it's through difficulties that we learn and grow, so why should we resent and resist them? Practice gratitude for everything, good and bad.

Kindness

How strange to think of kindness as a practice. Isn't it obvious? I think most of us want to be kind. It's easy to forget. Especially when we are angry and frustrated, or when someone else mistreats us or causes us pain, loss, or disgrace, such as when another driver suddenly cuts in front of us in traffic or we get a bad review at work. Then our anger flares up, and we sometimes yell, blame, judge, and mistreat in turn. Instead, when these emotions and impulses arise, notice them, don't suppress them, let them go, and be kind. Practice kindness when it's hard to do so. And don't forget to practice kindness even toward yourself. Often this can be the most challenging.

I taught a mindfulness workshop at Facebook headquarters recently. As we prepared for three minutes of mindfulness meditation, I said to the participants, "You can do this either the easy way or the easier way. The easy way is to follow your breathing or to count your exhalations. The easier way is to just sit quietly." After we did this, someone commented, "When I get distracted and stop following my breath, I feel guilty, as though I have failed." I thanked the person and said that this was an important recognition. Being distracted is part of mindfulness and part of daily life. And so are feeling guilty and judging ourselves. When you notice you are distracted, or that you are judging yourself, use this as an opportunity to practice kindness.

Compassion

This is the practice of actively seeking to relieve the pain and suffering of loved ones, friends, and other people, and it applies to our own suffering as well. Empathy and compassion are basic human traits. The other day a friend of mine was walking toward me. When she was about twenty feet away, she stumbled on a curb and lost her balance. In that moment, as I watched her, my body also felt out of balance. Without and beyond any thinking, I could feel the impending pain of her fall. This empathetic reaction was as automatic as the compassionate one that followed: I lunged toward her to attempt to soften her landing. Luckily, she caught herself and regained her balance in time. Compassion is such a natural, built-in human response. At the same time, our fears, our busyness, and our judgments can cover over this response and lead us to feel separate and alone. Thus, one antidote to our feelings of separation and isolation, to our moments of neediness and disconnection, is to practice helping others.

Sympathetic Joy

This is such a simple and powerful practice. So often we get caught up comparing ourselves with others: analyzing who's ahead and who's behind, and becoming envious of anyone who seems richer, better, luckier, smarter, or more talented. When you recognize these feelings and reactions, practice sympathetic joy instead. Notice the joy of others and celebrate it. This practice, and it does take practice, is consciously feeling the happiness of others — hearing a child laughing, seeing a loving couple smiling at each other in a restaurant, reading the announcement of a coworker's promotion. Whatever is happening in your life, whatever you feel you may lack, this practice is always available. For one day, practice sympathetic joy with everyone you meet. Notice what happens, in yourself and others.

Taking Responsibility

There are many actions that undermine equanimity. Blame is at the top of the list. Equanimity could even be defined as the practice of noticing blame, letting go of it, and transforming it with personal responsibility. Blame is the cause of so much unhappiness, whether we are blaming others or ourselves. Blame is finding fault in order to criticize, shame, or punish. This is useless and undermining. It never solves the problem at hand, while invariably sowing unhappiness, discord, misunderstandings, resentment, separation, conflict, and even violence.

When things go wrong, we understandably want to find the cause, but we can remember that we are all board-carrying fellows: everyone's perspective is limited, incomplete. We can never see the whole picture; no one can. Everyone involved in a situation also has an influence on it, whether directly or indirectly. When we feel the urge to blame, we can practice dropping judgment and instead focus on taking responsibility.

Often blaming happens so quickly and automatically that we don't even notice. I remember the time that my wife asked me for a recommendation for a designer for a project she was working on. I quickly wrote down the names of two designers that I often worked with and included short evaluations of each designer, naming their strengths and weaknesses. Then, without thinking, I sent my evaluations via email to the designers instead of to my wife. This was one of those *oops* moments. Though I didn't say anything very negative about either designer, my note was not intended for them to see. The moment I realized my mistake, I felt blame arise: "If only my wife hadn't asked me for this referral..." Noticing this reaction, I was surprised at myself. Without any hesitation, I was almost instinctually trying to shift responsibility and hide my own embarrassment over my error. But my wife was not to blame. This was a clear-cut instance of misplaced blame, and I quickly let the feeling go. Far more difficult are situations in which someone else's words or actions do directly cause us harm (emotional or otherwise).

The first step in reducing the tendency to blame others is to identify blaming whenever it arises: stop, notice, and label your reaction as blame. Just notice, then pause before acting or responding. Next, before you explain to the other people all the things they did wrong, ask yourself: "How did I contribute to this situation? Was it 1 percent, or more?" Take responsibility for that contribution, and use that as a basis for taking useful action. Turn that around if you are blaming yourself. Ask: "Am I the only one who contributed to this situation? Was my part 99 percent, or less?" If after doing this you still struggle with understanding who's at fault in a situation, do the "opposite perspectives" exercise in chapter 4 (page 80). Explore the statement "It's not my fault, but it is my responsibility." Even when we or others do something harmful, numerous circumstances conspire toward and culminate in that action; some are within our control and some are outside of anyone's control. Taking responsibility is a way of identifying the things we can control and the useful actions we can take and opening to new possibilities.

Letting Go

Equanimity is sometimes described as the practice of letting go. This is easier to talk about than to do. Letting go is a skill that takes practice. Emotions reside in the body; you might say our emotional attachments are literally embodied in us. Reacting to them is a powerful, ingrained habit; sometimes our reactions are automatic, instinctual fight-or-flight responses. It's important to emphasize that letting go is not about avoiding or denying our unhelpful emotions or attachments. It's about recognizing them as they occur and developing the ability to let them go: to simply release distraction, blame, fear, the busyness in our minds. We can learn this skill through attention training, through working with the whole mind and body, and by practicing letting go again and again.

Meditation practice can be described as the practice of letting go with each breath. With each exhale, explore really exhaling fully, letting go, really not knowing what will happen next. This is the practice of letting go of everything. Pausing throughout the day can be a useful way to practice letting go. When you start your car, pause, take a breath, and let go. Do this when you arrive at work or are about to begin a meeting, or any time the thought pops into your head. Let go and be curious.

There are many contexts in which to practice letting go. As a way to work with and develop equanimity, let's focus on three.

LETTING GO OF DISTRACTIONS: A good place to start to reduce distractions is compiling your not-to-do list. This is a useful list to keep, a companion to your list of tasks and projects. Write down the things that cause distractions, the things you should not be doing: perhaps, Web surfing, eating junk food, having long, detailed conversations about topics you don't need to know the details to. However you define distractions, list them, then pay attention and notice. Sometimes it can help to look at what we are avoiding and not getting to. What is it that prevents you from getting done what is important or essential? Is this a form of distraction?

LETTING GO OF UNDERMINING EMOTIONS: Paying attention to your emotional life is the starting point for this practice. Pause, notice, label. What are you feeling? Just notice your reactions and responses. If impatience is an issue for you, focus on noticing and letting go of impatience. The point is not to avoid impatience, or even to lessen it, but to uncover all the places it occurs and guides our actions, and then to insert a breathing space in which we decide how to respond differently. The same practice can be used for anger, jealousy, and any of the eight imprisonments.

LETTING GO OF WORRY: The most powerful way to let go of worry and anxiety about the future is to find ways to be more present. Begin by noticing worry and anxiety anytime you are thinking about what might happen, planning, or fretting about the future. Label these thoughts and emotions as worry: "Here comes worry....These feelings are just worry arising." Then practice attention training — come back to your body and breath, to your sensations, and examine what you see and hear inside. What other feelings are arising?

Joy of Being

As you do with gratefulness, practice the joy of being every day. Every time you think of it, for one breath, just be. Create some routines and rituals to assure that you have at least some "being" time each day — a daily meditation practice, a walk outside during lunchtime, a few minutes of reading poetry to yourself in the afternoon. Explore the art and practice of moving from attainment to nonattainment, from doing and getting to just being. We are such doers. It is easy to turn mindfulness, meditation, and yoga into another activity of doing. Notice this, be kind to yourself, and see if you can shift your approach. Reduce and, when possible, eliminate your unnecessary expectations. What relief! Let yourself experience beyond right and wrong, good and bad, beyond comparing, assessing, and analyzing.

Every situation presents an opportunity for learning, for increasing awareness, and for awakening to joy. Expanding your awareness — about yourself, and in relationship to others and to the world — is like breaking open a treasure chest. You don't need to do anything. The light of appreciation, the power of your emotional and cognitive gifts, and feelings of profound joy stop being blocked and can flow more freely.

Minding the Gap

A useful equanimity practice is noticing gaps between appearances and reality. I think we do this all the time, but we don't like to stay with it and learn from these gaps. I'm often surprised by the gaps in people and companies, between appearances and reality. So often, we put a good face on our own troubles, and we tend to believe (and react to) the appearances shown by others, especially those who appear successful, happy, sustainable. I've learned that when you look more deeply — what I sometimes call looking under the hood of a business or a person — you may unexpectedly notice a broken radiator or oil leaking from the engine. Todd's story is an excellent example of this, as I never would have guessed all the challenges he was facing in his life before he told me.

Seeing Challenges as Opportunities

Though "see challenges as opportunities" is a cliché, that doesn't make it less useful. I think that most of us need to be reminded to do this, over and over again. We all want things, and yet obstacles, challenges, and difficulties always seem to get in our way. It's frustrating. But according to the cultural myth of the hero's journey, there is no way to get what we want except by going through (and learning from) the inevitable challenges we will face. Further, if we resist an obstacle — if we want a promotion that we don't get and then sink into self-blame — we only cause ourselves suffering and distress without taking useful action. And, really, what is the difference? Whatever we label an experience — as a challenge or an opportunity — it is multidimensional. Our label just signals whether we are resisting or embracing the full breadth of our experience.

For instance, our nation's current economic crisis is certainly a challenge. There is nothing pretty about unemployment and people losing their homes. These things are painful. And yet, if we embrace the challenges that life presents to us — whether we asked for them or not — then we are making the most of what happens to us. We are learning to handle painful financial hardship with equanimity; perhaps we are learning to make different financial choices. Being a human being is fraught with challenges, small and large. Name some of yours. Identify the opportunities within these challenges, and reach for those.

Being Less Predictable

Certain Buddhist writings advise being less predictable. I find it very interesting, since it can be interpreted in many ways. First, in what ways are you predictable? We develop all kinds of routines, habits, and preferences. Some of them are quite healthy and recommended in this book: exercising regularly, meditating daily, developing an ongoing writing practice, and so on. Are we meant to undo these good routines? I don't think so. Instead, I think this advice is a guard against laziness, against unthinking torpor, against short-sightedness. Like embracing paradox, it's a way to wake us up, so we act in ways that are fresh and alive and open to new growth and possibility. Equanimity, like moderation, can sound boring, the exact opposite of the open-ended, risk-taking curiosity that not knowing is meant to cultivate. Notice how predictable your thinking and your responses can be, and play the trickster with yourself. Eat foods you don't like, wake up earlier or stay up late, read different kinds of books and see different kinds of movies. Explore your habits and assumptions. Play. Be curious. Say yes when you usually say no; get a different haircut. Unpredictableness is another good habit to cultivate.

Not Expecting Applause

We all want to be noticed. We all want to be accepted and loved. But our attachment to praise and a good reputation is what makes these part of the eight dilemmas. By expecting or needing applause, we set ourselves up for pain if we don't get it, or if we are not recognized in the way we desire. So notice when you expect applause, at work and at home. Just notice. Then, see if you can reduce or let go of the expectation. Can you find satisfaction in a job if you aren't rewarded with attention? Practice the opposite response: instead of silently hoping to be noticed, ask for applause. Can you ask for recognition with love and joy in your heart, rather than judgment or hurt feelings? Of course, it's wonderful to be applauded for what we do. It's even more wonderful to receive it when we don't expect it. Can you recognize and acknowledge your own efforts and feel satisfied in what you have accomplished? Can you have compassion for the hunger in you for praise and let it go?

Patience

Patience is another one of those austere, eat-it-because-it's-good-for-you words. We want to act, solve, work, build, and patience asks us to wait. Patience sounds like the dutiful opposite of freedom, creativity, and fun. No one wants to be told to be patient. I don't. And yet it is a powerful practice for developing equanimity. It is an antidote to anxiety, worry, doubt, excitement, and all the other impulses that would make us rush, that encourage us to skip all the boring stuff in the middle and read the last page to see how everything ends. People who work with natural rhythms — like farmers, winemakers, and doctors — know from experience that certain activities must be allowed to happen in their own time: planting when it is time to plant, harvesting when time to harvest, and giving the body time to heal. The work in this book has its own rhythm, too. Between the question and the solution is the doing, and what's in the middle is essential to the outcome. Learning to pause and notice oneself is part of that rhythm; it's a way of stopping, of practicing patience. Listening requires patience. In business and personal life, developing a plan, building a team, building a brand, and raising capital require patience (or are improved by it).

However, practicing patience doesn't mean that you always move slowly or that you become hesitant. Sometimes we need to move quickly and decisively; when events move fast, we have to move equally fast to keep up with them. Farmers and doctors also know when time is of the essence, when a quick response is the difference between success and failure, life and death.

That said, another aspect to the practice of patience is physically slowing down and moving less quickly. Notice when you feel under pressure to respond, and instead pause and take three breaths. Find the proper rhythm for every action and decision;

allow it to emerge, rather than forcing it. Then, if it comes time to sprint or act decisively, you do so from a place of calmness, deliberation, and clarity.

Already Broken

The great Thai monk Achaan Cha was famous for holding up a teacup and saying, "To me this cup is already broken." Everything is like this. Everything is beautiful and, simultaneously, everything is already broken. This is the truth of impermanence.

We don't like to look at the world in this way. We want to hold on to and protect everything we love, and to discard or turn away from everything that is broken. When something breaks, or a person leaves us or someone dies, we are completely upset, and we want to move away from the experience of loss as quickly as possible. Loss reminds us that the world isn't a safe place, so we try to protect the things we still possess more diligently; we hold on to relationships more tightly. We become stressed, paranoid, out of balance.

We tend to overlook the exquisite beauty of our imperfections. Broken is the nature of things. It is the nature of ourselves, especially ourselves. If we can embrace this, we can more fully appreciate our life, appreciate the preciousness of who we are and what we are, fully accept what comes to us and what leaves us. Whatever comes to us is a gift, a temporary gift. Whatever leaves us is also a gift, even when it is painful and we grieve deeply. What may be most difficult to grasp is that nothing exists that is not already broken from the start.

So, to embody equanimity, one of the most important practices is to treat our cup, and the offerings of the world, as already broken. Waking up this morning, I am now older than I was yesterday. Everyone and everything is. And yet, I just go about my

day, my routines, worries, and concerns, without really appreciating this fact. We may succeed in some aspect of our lives and feel
happy, content. We may think: Wonderful, now I have the job, or
the income, or the spouse, or the home that I want, and I don't
need to worry about that again. But then tomorrow, or a few days
later, or a few years later, loss arrives and we are confronted with
brokenness again.

"This teacup is already broken" is a wonderful paradox that
is meant to wake us up, so we see the ephemerality of life more
clearly and accurately — and appreciate how emotions and
equanimity walk hand in hand, and how by accepting both we
can live with more compassion, kindness, and effectiveness. This
leads to an abiding joy in being that's deeper than any day-to-day
happiness.

Experiment with seeing things as already broken. This book
will one day be in a recycling bin; it will become dust. So will all
your books, your computer, your car. Ultimately, everything that
is made and everyone who is born will eventually break down
and come to an end. This may seem like the ultimate downer. But
avoiding or denying this fact doesn't make it less true, doesn't
make you more effective; it leaves you more easily hurt, surprised,
and unbalanced by the inevitable breakdowns. The other truth is,
if you are alive, you are not broken entirely, and the world renews
itself constantly. Embodying equanimity means accepting and
embracing this bittersweet process, and finding balance within
it. Whether the teacup in your hand is broken today or not, can
you see the beauty of the teacup, broken and unbroken — of the
beauty of the sky, of the people around you, of yourself? Does
this help you appreciate the beauty and magnificence of everything in this moment just as it is?

Resistance Is Inevitable

I recently had dinner with a good friend in San Francisco who is a successful businesswoman and media consultant, as well as a mindfulness teacher. We were discussing the rise of mindfulness practice in general and in the corporate world, when at one point she stated emphatically, "I don't think mindfulness is really going to catch on or be the next big thing."

"Really?" I responded. "Why do you feel that way?"

She looked serious and said, "The problem is that when most people begin practicing mindfulness, they first become aware of their current pain and unhappiness. You and I know, from having a long-term mindfulness practice, that this is a stage, and that we all need to go through this. I don't think most people are going to be willing to stay with mindfulness practice if it involves facing and feeling the pain and discomfort that exist in your life right now. Who wants that!"

If you've read this far, you'll know that my friend was right: mindfulness involves looking squarely at our most difficult issues and feelings, some of which we may have spent many years avoiding. In fact, mindfulness often causes us to realize with some shock that our teacup is indeed already broken, and at first this can make us feel worse. Despite its rewards, bringing more attention and awareness to our work and our life brings this risk. Often the act of looking more closely at what we are doing, our feelings, the quality of our interactions, can be painful and disturbing. It is easy to become stuck in a work situation or a relationship or a life where we fall asleep or become numb. The act of waking up to the reality of our situation can be upsetting, even shocking. Yet waking up to what is, I believe, is always better than remaining asleep, to pretending that everything is okay when it is not.

Noticing and naming is an important step toward finding real joy and real freedom.

If, in doing this work, you find yourself resisting, or wondering if there must be some easier way, it's okay. Everyone resists; everyone struggles. When you do, practice kindness, compassion, and patience with yourself, and pick the work back up tomorrow. I think that almost everyone wants to feel good. There is tremendous evidence that happiness is the default state of human beings, and we have powerful social and genetic tendencies toward kindness and compassion. Yet there is no avoiding difficulty, no avoiding feeling pain, discomfort, anxiety, and loss. Naturally, we try: we grasp for happiness and try to avoid pain and loss, and soon find ourselves caught within the eight imprisonments. Mindfulness practice allows us to free ourselves by choosing differently. Paradoxically, we embrace all emotion, all our striving, emptiness, and loss, so we can act from a sense of equanimity, compassion, and caring for a world already broken.

These five paradoxes, or truths, are tools and practices for training ourselves to be more free — to widen our awareness and to take a different approach. We neither indulge in or cling to the comfort we seek nor repress the more difficult emotions that we tend to push away. With this shift, we are changed, and so the world is changed. I'm reminded of a famous story: a king assigns a brilliant builder to cover his entire kingdom with leather. He wants to cover all the rocks and pebbles so his feet won't feel the pain when he walks about the kingdom. Instead, the builder designs the king leather shoes. The world changes when we change our experience of it.

Many years ago, Shunryu Suzuki, founder of the San Francisco Zen Center and author of *Zen Mind Beginner's Mind*, was leading a traditional, seven-day Zen meditation retreat. These retreats involve a good deal of sitting meditation and a rigorous schedule from early in the morning till late at night. They provide an environment for people to deeply touch, and let go of, many experiences, identities, fears, and emotions. At one point, Suzuki-roshi was sitting with the retreat participants. He looked at the fifty men and women, broke the silence, and said, "The difficulty that you are experiencing right now..."

He paused. One of my friends, Zen teacher and writer Ed Brown, was there, and Ed said in that moment, after days of meditating and facing the difficulties of life as well as painful knees, legs, and back from sitting for so long, he imagined everyone in the room anticipated some words of relief or escape, some possibility of feeling transformed, or at least better. Then Suzuki continued, "...you will have for the rest of your life."

I believe this stunning, paradoxical remark, though it may have sparked some momentary despair, was Suzuki's way of encouraging people to explore and practice complete and radical acceptance. His teaching is simply to be present for whatever you are experiencing — the pains and difficulties, the joys and ease. Just show up completely, without wanting, wishing, or hoping that your situation will be different. This kind of presence is, in itself, transformative. With complete acceptance of what is, joy and freedom arise.

Chapter 8

BENEFIT OTHERS, BENEFIT YOURSELF

EFFECTIVENESS

*A true measure of your worth includes all the benefits
others have gained from your success.*

— CULLEN HIGHTOWER

I founded the company Brush Dance with the vision and inspiration of turning trash into beautiful greeting cards and wrapping paper. I aspired to help solve a significant environmental problem while creating a successful business. I knew that discarded paper makes up more than 28 percent of all landfill in the United States, creating literal mountains of waste. I aspired to bring more awareness to this problem, present a solution, and create a model for a financially sustainable business that took care of its employees, customers, and stakeholders.

I had a vision and took action to grow a business. As in the story of the three bricklayers in the prologue, my motivations were many, and sometimes competing. I wanted the freedom and flexibility of owning my own company. I wanted to earn a living and be able to take care of myself and my family. I wanted to build a management team and a company that could have significant impact, more than I could by myself. I wanted to be financially independent. I aspired to create wealth so that I could have more freedom in my own life and to invest in other companies that were helping to solve significant social issues. I wanted to demonstrate to myself and others that it was possible to lead a company with a sense of drive, urgency, and business savvy as well as with heart and compassion. In order to grow the business and have the impact I sought, I raised investment capital from family, friends, and "angel" investors, and I borrowed money from banks.

Brush Dance was one of the first companies in the world to create wrapping paper and greeting cards from recycled paper. In 1989 recycled paper was a new idea and had a negative reputation among printers. There were only a handful of paper mills in the United States that were capable of manufacturing recycled paper. I couldn't imagine the future we live in now, in which recycling is a daily habit, and recycled products of all kinds, including the book in your hands, are commonplace and eagerly promoted. And yet there remains much work to be done on this front.

Still, I remember the day when our first shipment of wrapping paper arrived. The company was in my home. A large truck came down the steep hill of my street and slowly backed into my driveway. The driver unlatched the truck door, and there were twenty cartons containing four different designs of recycled wrapping paper. I was excited. Then my heart sank. *Wrapping paper? Why are we making wrapping paper? Does the world really need wrapping paper?* This was a great question, and to this day I don't have a satisfying answer.

In that moment, I said to myself, "Yes, people need, use, and love wrapping paper. It is an expression of care. It not only holds the gift given but demonstrates special attention, a sense of beauty, and caring."

Perhaps, in my desire to start and grow a business, I succumbed to rationalizing. Perhaps, despite my doubts, I was right all along. The only thing I know for sure is that this was a powerful lesson in balancing intention and action, and vision and product, and experiencing the complex, paradoxical ways that benefiting others and benefiting ourselves are wound into the tightrope we walk every day.

BENEFIT OTHERS, BENEFIT YOURSELF
ACTION PLAN

This chapter helps you to define what gives your life meaning and then identify actions to support that vision. Like creating a business plan in chapter 6 (page 162), drafting vision statements is something you may do only periodically, but doing so provides a focus that will guide your decisions daily, even moment to moment. Ultimately, these practices and activities help us align our intentions with our actions, our means with our ends, so we live right now the beneficial life we desire.

1. Ask yourself: What do I call the world? Write down, or draw visually, the spheres in your life that are most meaningful (page 221).

2. Write down how you feel you currently impact or influence these worlds in a positive way, or create an "impact diagram" (page 222).

3. Separately, write down or consider what negative impacts or influences you might be having in the world (page 223).

4. Draft multiple vision statements for all the ways you would most like to benefit others and impact the world (page 228).

5. Create an informal, one-page business plan for each statement, which lists the actions you will pursue (page 228).

6. Rephrase your vision statements as persuasive offerings (page 230).

7. Consider how in your relationships you can lead by influence (page 232).

8. Check the climate of your workplace or business (page 232).

9. To benefit yourself, take care of your physical health (page 243).

10. To become aware of your self-talk, explore your voices (page 246).

11. To improve your sense of community and connection, have more real conversations (page 250) and participate in small groups (page 250).

12. Care for and shape your personal brand (page 251).

13. Practicing saying yes to yourself, your work, others, and the world (page 255).

BENEFIT OTHERS

What Do You Call the World?

There is a famous story from the Zen tradition about two teachers meeting on the road.

One teacher asks the other, "Where do you come from?"

The second replies, "From the south."

The first asks, "How is Zen practice in the south these days?"

The second responds, "There is lots of discussion."

The first states, "How can all the discussion compare to planting the fields and cooking rice?"

The second asks, "What are you doing about the world?"

The first replies, "What do you call the world?"

This dialogue not only reminds me of discussions I hear in the world of business, nonprofits, and social entrepreneurship but represents an ongoing dialogue I have with myself. Is the work I'm doing helping others? Am I focused on the critical problems, the right problems? Are my efforts and actions aligned with my purpose and vision? All these questions arose for me as I looked at my first batch of wrapping paper, and they continue to arise every single day.

During my time running Brush Dance, I was aware that I was living on a tightrope and balancing multiple, sometimes competing, agendas — improving the world and taking care of me, constantly driving change and accepting what is. At times, it was complex and amazingly confusing. At times, utterly simple and clear — just take the next step, plan the next new product, have the next conversation. Make sure there is enough money in the bank to pay payroll. When the phone rings, answer it, whether it is from a paper supplier wondering when it will be paid, an artist with an idea for a new greeting card series, or a customer telling me the story of how one of our greeting cards was the perfect birthday gift that touched the heart of her dying mother.

This Zen story asks, Where are we putting our focus and attention? What is right and appropriate action? Are we doing the things that matter? Today, I work primarily with business leaders, but what about all the other types of populations and communities? What about the homeless people I see in the streets of San Francisco every day? What's more important: food or spiritual sustenance? Helping those who create jobs or those who need jobs? As the story implies, there is no single, inherent right answer, and as individuals our resources are limited. We have to make choices, and as we know from the state of our own political discourse, universal agreement on how to solve the world's problems doesn't exist. Like the teachers in the story, we must define and answer these essential questions on our own terms: What do I call the world? How can I take care of that world? What am I actually doing? Once we've answered those, the next questions are: Could I be doing more? How can I have the most impact? How can I best leverage my time and resources?

We all want to live a life that has meaning and purpose, that makes a positive difference. By most definitions, "meaningful" work is whatever fulfills some larger purpose, some higher calling, that is more than just taking care of ourselves. We find meaning in helping others, by improving the world we all share. The executives and leaders I coach all desire this sense of purpose and suffer if they feel it lacking. They also question whether they are serving that larger purpose in the best, most effective ways. The first step in figuring that out, as the Zen story implies, is defining what we mean by "the world."

There are, in fact, many worlds that we are involved in and

strive to take care of. We work hard to take care of the world of our family. We are connected to the world of our friends and our communities, the world of our body, the world of spirit. Each individual relationship is like its own world. Every organization and workplace is its own world. Sometimes each moment, each experience, can seem like its own world, when we slow down enough to notice.

Ask yourself right now: What worlds am I part of? Which am I actively serving? Which are most important to me? In a journal or on a piece of paper, name these worlds in as much detail and specificity as you can. Order them by your own subjective sense of importance. If it helps you to visualize this, create a diagram of your universe of worlds. As with a word cloud, make the most important worlds bigger and the less important ones smaller (irrespective of what others may think or how many people they involve). Be expansive in this list; note worlds within worlds. And don't neglect the world of pausing and everyday life: of planting a garden and cooking rice, of appreciating beauty, celebrating good fortune, mourning loss, raising children, caring for the sick, and more. What about all these? Aren't they as important and vital as the public arenas we typically look to for validation and purpose — such as our jobs and workplaces?

Ultimately, why is it that we want to live more effective, balanced, healthy, and happy lives? To what purpose? This chapter raises these questions; it helps you name these meaningful endeavors and then see how to bring your values and actions into alignment. Inevitably, this raises tricky issues of context and control — of how much our worlds are self-defined and how much they are defined for us, of what we can influence and what is beyond our influence.

For the moment, let's stay with the first question: What do you call the world? Recall the story of the three bricklayers: by describing what they saw as their job, they each defined the world that mattered to them, the focus that gave the work meaning. One focused on making the building itself; the second focused on the well-being of family; the third focused on creating a gathering place for spiritual worship. All were engaged in the same activity, but the meaning of it, each person's vision of its impact, was utterly different. By naming worlds, you are also naming the ways you would like to have impact. In the end, there are no lesser or more important impacts. The bricklayer who focuses on making the building well is impacting the business that hired him or her as well as every person who uses the building: ensuring it is safe and structurally sound, pleasing to the eye and enduring. Are these impacts any less profound than those of the bricklayer whose main motivation is that the building be a cathedral? The world needs farmers to grow the food that sustains us, and truckers and highways to get that food to stores. We need teachers and therapists, businesspeople and priests. And the impacts of all these jobs and roles radiate through our entire society.

To help see this for yourself, once you define your worlds, take a moment to note and trace impacts. Simply write about this or, if it helps to visualize, create an impact diagram, almost like a map. Identify who is affected by your most important worlds, and your work in them, and who is affected by those you impact. Look upstream as well as downstream: which people and organizations impact your life? Who provides you with food, technology, clothing, services? How does what you do affect them? Begin to see the interconnected web of relationships, worlds, and impacts that you actually are a part of. Yes, the closer you look, the more complexity and interconnection grows to an almost infinite degree. Keep naming and tracing till your perspective is as wide as possible.

Real Life: The Devil's Bargain

As I hope the exercise above demonstrates, we each live within an amazingly complex, multilayered web of connections. Within that, our task is to decide how to make a living, what communities to join or create, what impacts to have, and how to create joy and satisfaction in our lives. But what happens when our dreams, goals, and hopes meet the practical world? As we all know, good intentions are not enough to ensure success, and our actions can sometimes have consequences that turn our hopes inside out. The day-to-day world is a dynamic, quickly changing, and challenging place. War, famine, overpopulation, climate change, poverty, recession, crime, oppression: all of these things are disturbing realities in the world. While we name worlds and the positive impacts we would like to have, we also must open our eyes to the negative impacts we may also be having. As we move forward, pursuing meaning and purpose in our lives, realize that one of the most difficult paradoxes we face is that even our most noble acts may cause pain for some, and even within our most terrible mistakes, good can occur. Naming our impacts, and doing our best to minimize negative ones, is an important aspect of effectiveness.

Here is a concrete example of this tension, this paradox and dilemma, from my own life. At one point, Brush Dance increased sales of writing journals, and I wanted to increase production to meet demand as well as expand the company's line of journals. I discovered that it was not possible to be in the journal business and manufacture journals in the United States or Canada. Supporting US workers seemed like an honorable and sensible intention, but the economics did not work to continue doing so for

Brush Dance's journal business. What I discovered was that in order to sell journals at a competitive price, we had to make them in China. And yet, this was a time when China was being accused of human rights violations, and I was concerned about supporting the Chinese government, even tangentially, as well as the environmental costs of shipping products across the ocean. However, after extensive research, we began producing our journal line in China.

I met with a colleague who had visited the plant in China and learned that the company we were working with treated its employees well and paid them fairly, at least in the context of China's economy. However, when my teenage daughter noticed that our journals were made in China, she gave me a stern lecture, questioning and doubting the alignment of my values and business practices. Sometime after this, at a trade show in New York, I met with the Chinese company's representatives, who were all women in their thirties and forties. I spoke about my concerns about making products in China. They were quite puzzled and surprised. One said to me, "We are just people, with the intention of growing a business in the best way we know. We have children and families to feed. We are not the Chinese government and don't condone all the actions of the Chinese government, just as you are not the US government, nor do we question doing business with you because of the actions of your government."

As the women brought home to me, impacts differ depending on your perspective, and the political misgivings I expressed can cut both ways. And just to be clear: I mention China only as an example, not to single out any one nation. Then again, we are each complicit in whatever the impacts of our actions are, and those impacts will always be imperfect, mixed. You may not be facing the challenging question of where to manufacture your company's products. However, nearly everyone buys or uses goods manufactured in countries whose politics and government we may not agree with. We realize our "devil's bargain" when we pay attention to where our most precious everyday objects are made — our computers, phones, cars, books, tables, chairs, silverware, and so on. Then there is the energy that powers our cars, warms our houses, and moves our food to stores — the oil we import from a wide range of countries across the globe. How is this energy we use affecting the changing environment we all share? If our job helps create better technology, such as faster and quicker ways for people to communicate with each other, is this helping or hurting our everyday sense of connection? I work with a scientist who helps create drugs to treat diseases, but I sometimes wonder — do these drugs that treat diseases reduce or distract from efforts to actually cure the diseases?

On a more intimate level, we are constantly challenged to evaluate the impacts of our choices on our closest communities — our family and circle of friends. If, like the second bricklayer, our main desire with our work is to care for the well-being of our family, is our job laying bricks the best way to do that? If we are paid poorly and are rarely home, then the negative impacts may outweigh the positive. It is useful to question and examine whether our actions are aligned with our values, and if the means of our lives undermine our stated ends. Refer back to Harry Roberts's three questions: What do you want? What do you have to do to get it? Can you pay the price? Only with this information can we know when to move ahead confidently and when we need to be more inquisitive, when to fight for change and when to accept things as they are. When to speak up and when to be silent. When to be like the orchestra leader, taking a wide view of all the instruments, and when to pick up our instrument and play our own important and particular notes.

Creating Alignment

When it comes to benefiting others, there is no shortage of paradox. As I've said, I'm not seeking paradox; I want clarity. Yet the way to clarity and alignment is often through embracing paradox. I founded Brush Dance as an environmentally conscious business making recycled-paper products, but if I was shipping journals from overseas, at what point would the negative environmental impacts of this manufacturing process outweigh the benefits of the product itself? Did I need to make small changes and marginal improvements to be satisfied; did I need to radically rethink our manufacturing process (and perhaps impact the business's potential profit); or did I need to quit the recycled-paper business altogether as unviable, or impossible to align with my stated goals?

Others most likely would have made different decisions than I did, and I made different decisions at different times as circumstances changed. I revisited this question of environmental impact continually, and the company devised new solutions at every turn. It was a process of trial and error, with no easy-to-follow steps, no clear recipes. In one sense, it was sometimes exhausting to always be questioning the company's basic mandate; it was always disappointing to find that, yet again, we were falling out of alignment. On the other hand, that's life. We find a good balance, things change, and we must find our balance again.

This chapter and this book are meant as a manual to help you successfully walk the paradoxical tightropes of your life. Yet while there are effective methods for doing this, you must take the specific steps that are right for you. There is no single recipe; your life makes up the ingredients. How you combine and cook them is up to you. What are you cooking, what are your resources and circumstances, and what are the challenging paradoxes this raises? See the paradoxes and embrace them; by exploring them you will find more clarity, and you can then take effective, meaningful action that benefits others. This is how, in our own individual ways, we each take care of the world.

Vision, or the Problem You Want to Solve

Figuring out the best way to benefit others begins with vision, with naming an intention or problem we want solved. Sometimes this arrives quietly and intuitively, other times in a flash of insight or inspiration.

I had lunch recently with a friend, writer Roger Housden. Roger described leading a poetry session recently for a group of veterans who had fought in Iraq and Afghanistan. When he was being introduced, he was asked to share his intention with the group; specifically, he was asked to share his "fierce intention." Roger paused at hearing these words and this question. "I don't have a fierce intention," he said. "I listen carefully and quietly to the deep intuitions, streams, and voices that quietly seep or noisily rumble through my body, my consciousness, my being." I was moved by this response. What I heard Roger saying, in part, is that vision is not completely a question of what problem you choose to solve. It's about being open and aware enough to notice what problem chooses you! Often it is the circumstances and events of life that provide openings and possibilities. I particularly liked that Roger turned this introduction into a teaching moment, both in how he responded and in what he said. He didn't try to fit himself into the question but instead redefined intention. Then he described his own process. In that moment, he was practicing and demonstrating the point he was making.

Above, you named the worlds you are part of, and you established a rough hierarchy of importance among them. You also considered the impacts you would like to have as well as the potential reach of your influence. Now, in your most important spheres, consider what you might actually do to benefit others. You can focus on only one world or tackle several or many, but be concrete and specific: What will you do and who will benefit — where, how, and when? Craft succinct statements of purpose like "I choose to benefit this part of the world by doing the following: _____. This will occur [in this place] when I [do this particular activity] [during this time frame]."

Describing this vision is very similar to creating the business plan I describe in chapter 6. However, the focus here is specifically on helping others. Also, I encourage you to do this for all the important relationships in your life: for the worlds of family, friends, and community, not just for work and business. How you phrase your vision statement isn't important. Just get it down on paper; nothing fancy. You may have several visions. Great. If you don't have a specific, concrete vision for how to help, simply stay with the question. Listen. Create enough time and space, even a small amount each day, listening to the questions and noticing what responds. As my friend Roger suggests, listen to the world. It will express its needs and show you the problems that need solving; it may even reveal the specific way you can address them.

I was first introduced to this method of listening and questioning during my MBA program at New York University. The professor of an entrepreneurship class gave this as a weekly assignment: begin noticing problems, identifying solutions, and visualizing how this could be a business or organization. Try this exercise, which I call the one-page business plan: Wherever you go, start seeing what problems exist in your world, large and small. Then, brainstorm possible solutions. In a single page, describe a problem, your solution, and the actions you would take. While you don't need to think in terms of starting a business or company, consider what help you might offer, whose help you might need, and how to enlist or organize that help. During business school, I noticed that by doing this I was training my mind, little by little, to see differently, to think differently — to see needs and visualize solutions. It was this way of thinking that led me to begin Brush Dance. I saw that environmental awareness would become a high priority in our world, and I noticed that the greeting card and wrapping paper business was enormous, and I saw that virtually no one was making these products from recycled paper. I founded my consulting practice, ZBA Associates, in the same way: I saw a need to help corporate and nonprofit leaders become more self-aware, more composed, and more focused as a way to more skillfully lead and solve important problems.

Solutions, or Presenting Your Offer

I have been running a one-person coaching and consulting company for more than eight years. One of my mentors recently asked me, "Do you know, really, what business you are in?" I thought this was a silly question; of course I knew the answer. I said I was an executive coach and leadership consultant. He responded, "I would say that you are a 100 percent commissioned salesperson." I was surprised and not happy to hear this, but before I could formulate my rebuttal, I recognized that he was correct. Not only was his statement accurate, but it provided a new and useful lens through which to view my business. You present an offer, a solution that solves a particular problem. Through ZBA, I provide a service, not a product, but I do have something to sell, what I like to call "my offer" and "solution." If someone doesn't "buy" my conception of the problem and the benefits I offer, then they won't engage my services.

This is an important concept for any company or organization, but it applies equally well to all aspects of our personal life. It is usually thought of as sales and marketing — crafting a convincing message about what you are selling. My problem with what my mentor said wasn't the underlying concept, but the negative connotations of the word *sell*. I find that shifting the language creates a powerful distinction. Instead of selling something, describe what you are offering. Think of the situation from the perspective of the person or community you want to help: What do they need and how will you provide that? What is your message? Do this with your vision statements. Reconsider them as offerings, and rephrase them as persuasive messages. In fact, we do this whenever we apply for a job: we try to encapsulate our talents, skills, and experience so they clearly fill the needs of the position we are applying for. By trying to help others, we are in essence applying for a job. Try this as an experiment: What are you offering? What is the problem you are solving? What are the benefits to your customers? What role will you fill?

Actions and Influence, or Developing the Means to an End

As with a traditional business plan, the heart of any offering lies in how you plan to actualize your vision, intention, and purpose. Moving from planning to acting; anticipating problems and challenges and rising to find creative solutions; tallying your resources and skills, and gathering any support you will need. Then, as you move forward, developing skillful attention: knowing when to be flexible, when to change course, and when to stand your ground. In business, particularly new ventures, success often hinges on how skillfully the business pivots to change course in response to new information and new opportunities.

So far, in naming your worlds and phrasing your offerings, you will have already named some of the actions you will take to benefit others. Sometimes these are implicit in your vision. Nevertheless, at this point, see if you can clarify next steps within your one-page business plan. While I can't advise you on what specific actions to take, I can offer some guidance about how to evaluate how well you are doing and whether you are having the sort of influence and impact you desire.

For when it comes to benefiting others, this process of reflection is essential. Developing healthy, reliable, cooperative relationships is often not just the vital means to an end but the end in itself. To have any positive impact, it is important to be skilled at teamwork and conscious of how we are using our influence. I don't remember there being any training, not even one word, about influencing people and teamwork during my two-year MBA program. And yet very little gets done unless we develop our own presence and awareness, our listening and speaking skills, our ability to respond to what is actually needed. In other words, our emotional intelligence. This is critical for interacting with others. Taking care of the world means working with other people, and this means influencing as well as being influenced by others. And this is the paradox of this particular insight: that in seeking to create change in the world we must allow ourselves to be changed. We must both lead and listen, be both flexible and persistent, and value the process as highly as any measurable achievements. Oftentimes, when it comes to benefiting others, how we enact change is as important as or more important than the change itself.

Here are three key practices of what I like to call "leading by influence."

EXAMINE YOUR INFLUENCE

With every action and outcome, ask yourself: What did I do or not do to make this happen? Everything you do and don't do, and everything you say and don't say, influences others. This is a subtle and important baseline assumption of building trust and of effective leadership. If you don't say something about someone's good effort or good result, this sends a message. Take off the blinders to how you influence others, to the messages you give. Let go of blaming others and looking for fault outside yourself. And make it a habit to ask others for their feedback: How were they influenced by you? What do they wish you'd done or not done?

In this way, you actively improve the process of working with others, and you demonstrate that you value the means as much as the ends.

CHECK THE CLIMATE

Every organization, company, community, and other group of people has a climate, which refers to the overall culture of the group. What's the climate like where you work, or in the worlds you are seeking to benefit? Is it open and collaborative? Is it closed, secretive, and political? Take the temperature of the group dynamics, and account for them. To what degree will the established dynamics help or hinder what you hope to accomplish? Is a dull or ineffective climate the thing that needs changing?

What would you like the climate to be, and what actions can you take to move it in that direction? This may sound simple and obvious, and yet I've noticed that very few organizations ask these questions and take effective action on a regular basis. Though there are countless values, relationships, and actions that contribute to climate, I find that three primary components are trust, meetings, and decision making. Though an entire book can be written on this subject, let's briefly explore these three areas.

TRUST: In organizations that build trust, people place a strong emphasis on aligning words and actions. People are encouraged to be open, transparent, and vulnerable. Expectations are clear. Nearly everyone knows what success looks like for individuals, teams, and the organization. Mistakes and failures are openly acknowledged and seen as a path toward finding solutions and increasing innovation. There is a high level of self-awareness and a strong emphasis on listening, building great teams, and collaboration. People feel valued for who they are and for the contributions they make.

MEETINGS: To foster a healthy climate, meetings are often times of learning, exchange, and enthusiasm. The purpose and expected outcomes are clear. There are a variety of types of meetings, and everyone involved knows what kind of meeting is being held: problem solving, information sharing, work planning, strategic planning, brainstorming, and so on. There is clear preparation and follow-through for all meetings. The right people are at the right meetings at the right times; not too many, not too few, just right.

DECISION MAKING: In organizations (and families) with healthy climates there is clarity about who makes what decisions. Healthy decision making is a result of a high level of trust and a culture of skillful meetings. There is an emphasis on freedom, autonomy, and responsibility — individuals feel free to ask difficult questions. People know what decisions are theirs to make and what decisions are made by others. There is a strong emphasis on personal and team responsibility.

Lead Change

Change begins by noticing the gaps between where you are and where you want to be, as well as identifying your own resistance and habits regarding change. What improvements would you like to see in the world or in your relationships? Make sure to embody those changes in yourself first. As Gandhi once said, be the change you want to see in the world. This is the most effective way to lead, and by leading, to benefit others. One way to begin is to say to yourself and to those you work with, "In the past, I didn't listen well (or plan well, or focus well, and so on). This is how I plan to be different moving forward. I value your feedback and hope you will help me."

Look at your vision statements and the ways you hope to help others. Do any of these represent gaps in your own personal life, work, or communication style? What in the present or in your past may have contributed to the situation as it now exists? If there are things, can you change them first? Explore making statements that specify these intentions: In the past I did this; moving forward I will be different by doing this.

Changing the Way Business Does Business

In the bestselling book *Blessed Unrest: How the Largest Social Movement in History Is Restoring Grace, Social Justice, and Beauty to the World*, Paul Hawken set out to count the number of organizations in existence working for environmental and social justice. He expected to find perhaps thirty thousand, then he increased his estimate to a hundred thousand. After extensive research he estimates that there are more than 2 million such organizations.

To benefit others, we first focus in the most personal terms, within the context of our life and relationships as we currently experience them. In the end, benefiting others is also about changing the world: changing our society's organizations and systems for the benefit of all of us. Capitalism as expressed by the unfettered pursuit of wealth without a social conscience is destructive and foolish. Look closely at US industry and business, and we find the unintended consequences of unfettered greed: unhealthy manufacturing, industrial, and food supply systems that are destructive to our environment, and thus to ourselves. We find an economic system that has created an imbalanced, unequal distribution of wealth, in which 1 percent of the population controls more than 30 percent of the country's wealth, and there is a persistent and growing underclass. The rules and assumptions of capitalism have been partial and one-sided; it values creating wealth over almost all other concerns. We freely spend the world's limited resources and undervalue our quality of life by harming the environment and negatively impacting human safety, health, and well-being. In essence, our current brand of capitalism fails to take into account all the real costs of doing business. What is the actual cost of removing natural resources from the earth, clear-cutting rain forests, and leveling mountains? It's time to change the game, time to rewrite the rules of business. It is my firm belief that, just as we can change our personal relationships, we can change the system and redefine the way we do business: it is indeed possible to enjoy all of the advantages of a free-market economy while maintaining a social conscience and a sensibility of stewardship, in which we also value taking care of people and the environment.

I see this already happening. As cited above, nonprofit entrepreneurship is flourishing. Even more intriguing, the world of for-profit social entrepreneurship is exploding. These are for-profit companies that are also committed to benefiting society. Nearly every major MBA program in the country now offers courses and training in this realm, in which the focus is on creating a company that balances making money with benefiting others. There are at least three major categories of for-profit companies that combine and integrate profit with social good: environmental, workplace, and finance.

Environmental Stewardship

These for-profit companies create products in ways that either benefit the environment or strive to not harm the environment. One example of an environmentally focused, socially responsible company is Patagonia, which makes clothing with great respect for the environment. I once heard Yvon Chouinard, Patagonia's founder and CEO, describe the challenge of making environmentally friendly clothing. His research unearthed that toxic chemicals were required to create orange-colored dyes. As a result, the company decided to stop producing all orange clothing, despite its popularity. Stonyfield Farms is a pioneer working with local farmers in producing organic yogurt and in developing ways to create healthy products while taking care of the environment. Seventh Generation was one of the first companies in the world to make environmentally friendly household products, and they continue to be a leader in the field. Today there are an enormous number of companies that could be cited for their environmental stewardship.

Workplace Health

This category of company includes those that have been outstanding in taking care of the health and well-being of their employees. Eileen Fisher, a clothing designer and manufacturer and retail store outlet, is one example. I have met Eileen Fisher and spent time with several of the company's senior executives. Here are some of the values and ways of doing business this company publicly proclaims on its website.

Communicate Openly

- Be present. Be accessible. Listen. Ask questions. Share information. Learn more about and respect other people's perspectives.
- Find your voice. Trust and express it. Share your own ideas. Integrate your thinking into the big picture. Be conscious of how your presence and style affect others.

Tell the Truth

- Be authentic. Tell the truth with great kindness.
- Be open about mistakes. We make them every day. In the middle of a mistake we discover a new solution. There are infinite opportunities to learn.

Nurture Growth in Others

- Support people in knowing their passions, strengths, and work styles. Celebrate who they are.

- Create a shared vision of each person's path. Develop shared expectations.
- Help people to set priorities and balance the varying elements of their work lives. Encourage them to seek new challenges and possibilities. Every person expands the company's potential.
- Support people to find meaningful ways to take care of themselves. Help people find ways to reduce stress.

Nurture Growth in Yourself

- Know yourself. Be yourself. Embrace your authentic style. Deepen and engage your strengths and passions — that's how you make the most valuable contribution.
- Identify where you want to grow. Stretch yourself. Value other people's gifts. Draw on them — they complement your own.
- Nurture your well-being. Model a balanced life and support others to do the same.

Create a Joyful Atmosphere

- Have fun every day. Focus on the positive. Inspire others to be positive.
- Discover the possibilities in each situation.
- Honor and celebrate our diversity. Together we create something wonderful.

Isn't this how most of us truly aspire to run our companies as well as live our lives? I'm aware that this is not easy. I'm not suggesting we see the world through rose-colored glasses, or that the company and the people who run it always live up to these ideals. They are not perfect. Who is? The best we can do, as the Eileen

Fisher company does, is to make a sincere effort to define values and to work in alignment with those values. To be both real and visionary, grounded in reality while aiming high.

The list of companies dedicated to creating healthy work environments is large and growing. Google, one of the largest companies on the planet, is such an example. Again, they are not perfect. People at Google work hard. Being surrounded by talented overachievers can be stressful. Google provides an amazing array of services for its employees: first of all, unlimited free food that is healthy, nutritious, and of the highest quality, along with on-site massage, meditation, a gym, dry cleaning, haircuts, car washing, and more. All are aimed at supporting and nurturing a healthy workforce.

Some people speculate the company's underlying intention is self-serving — providing perks that encourage people to work long hours and sacrifice their work/life balance. The company does expect a lot from its employees, and the company recognizes that, in turn, employees expect a lot from the company. When properly balanced and sincerely pursued, healthy workplace policies benefit everyone. I believe the motivations at Google and similar companies are many: to attract and retain talented people, to support people to focus on their work, and to nurture a healthy workforce that emphasizes high achievement drive and a collaborative environment.

Finance with Heart

Calvert Investments is a $12 billion company that focuses on socially responsible investments — investments in companies that are not involved in creating weapons, in manufacturing cigarettes, or in undermining the environment. In the financial services sector, integrating business and social responsibility is a growing trend.

As you might expect, Calvert doesn't just focus on investing in socially responsible companies; it tries to embody one itself. As it promises on its website: "Calvert embraces transparency and corporate responsibility in our own operations — which is demonstrated by our Corporate Sustainability Reports — and has been recognized for our community involvement and workplace policies by organizations as diverse as the Metropolitan Washington DC Council of Governments, the US Environmental Protection Agency, and *Working Mother* magazine."

New Resource Bank is another example; this for-profit bank based in San Francisco uses its deposits to make loans to those seeking low-income housing and for other socially responsible causes. As it says in its vision statement: "New Resource Bank is a mission-driven community bank focused on sustainability. We work to have positive environmental and social impacts, as well as make a profit, and we support businesses that do the same. We also serve sustainability-minded nonprofits and individuals."

Benefit Corporations

Newest to arrive is a new form of corporation, what's called a Benefit Corporation, or B Corp. This newly legal format is the result of a grassroots movement that has the potential to create an enormous impact in the business world and significant systemic change. By 2012, it was approved in only seven states, but it is expected to be available in many more states by the end of 2013. Traditionally, the definition of a typical for-profit corporation is that its primary responsibility is to maximize profits for its shareholders. A B Corp builds a different, wider responsibility into its corporate bylaws. A B Corp's mandate is to benefit its stakeholders and its customers. In essence it operates with not just one bottom line, profits, but with three bottom lines: people, planet, and profits.

. Here is an excerpt of the B Corp vision statement from its website.

> Our vision is simple yet ambitious: to create a new sector of the economy which uses the power of business to solve social and environmental problems. This sector will be comprised of a new type of corporation — the B Corporation — that meets rigorous and independent standards of social and environmental performance, accountability, and transparency.
>
> As a result, individuals will have greater economic opportunity, society will move closer to achieving a positive environmental footprint, more people will be employed in great places to work, and we will have built stronger communities at home and across the world.

Do good, avoid harm, and help others is the essential teaching of right livelihood in Zen Buddhism, as well as many religious traditions and systems of ethics. Isn't this common sense, and if so, why isn't this the essential basis of all business? How can we make a living and find satisfaction in our work while simultaneously helping others? To do this, it is important to transform the concept of business as being primarily about creating wealth for ourselves and to see business as the bricks out of which we build a healthy society that serves all of us. Seeking this balance is no longer an option but a necessity.

BENEFIT YOURSELF

We are all in this together. So when you realize
that you're talking to yourself, label it "thinking"
and notice your tone of voice. Let it be compassionate and
gentle and humorous. Then you'll be changing old stuck patterns
that are shared by the whole human race. Compassion for others
begins with kindness to ourselves.

— PEMA CHÖDRÖN

A student asks the teacher, "I'm feeling discouraged. What should I do?"

The teacher responds, "Encourage others."

Here again is the essence of this chapter's paradox: as Buddhist teacher Pema Chödrön says, compassion for others begins with expressing compassion for ourselves. Then again, according to this Zen dialogue, the path for healing our emotional suffering is to focus, not on ourselves, but on helping others. Within this circular logic is an essential truth about our human predicament: we are all in this together, and we succeed or fail together.

If we just take care of ourselves and ignore helping others, what meaning does our life have? We will harm the relationships and real connections that provide our lives with fulfillment and meaning. If we devote our lives to helping others but don't take care of ourselves, what good is that? We will be depleted, unhappy, or both, and soon become ineffective. Where is the balance? Again, balance is not achieved by finding a midpoint. It doesn't work to halfheartedly help others and halfheartedly take care of ourselves. The real question is: How can we fully take care of others and fully take care of ourselves at the same time? Let's explore this realm.

First Things First: Take Care of Your Health

I work with many busy, high-powered men and women. They are business and nonprofit leaders, as well as people outside the business world, who aspire to both take care of the world and take care of themselves. This is extremely challenging for a host of ancient and thoroughly modern reasons. News about the problems of our twenty-first-century world appears in the palm of our hands, and those problems seem to be mounting and increasingly complex: financial meltdowns, job insecurity, international conflicts, 24/7 information-technology overload, environmental crises. These are laid over the basic human conditions that challenge every generation: old age, sickness, and death, caring for one's family, raising children. And underlying all these circumstances are the challenges of self and what it means to be human: wrestling with the suffering in our hearts and trying to figure out who we are and what we are meant to do. That is, seeking to survive each day without succumbing to the self-defeating impulses of greed, hatred, and delusion.

During a recent Search Inside Yourself, Mindfulness and Emotional Intelligence Program I was teaching at Google's headquarters in Mountain View, I noticed that a number of people looked exhausted. I could see they were interested in the material, yet several were struggling to stay alert. It struck me that while we were teaching the art and practice of mindfulness, building emotional competencies, and skillful leadership, we weren't addressing, and were perhaps overlooking, some basic, important habits. Without proper self-care — without enough sleep, exercise, and healthy food — we undermine our efforts before we begin.

Is it strange to arrive at the end of this book to discuss physical health? This would seem to be the most basic step, and yet it appears last. In fact, that's often the way we treat our everyday well-being — making it our lowest priority, the last thing we make time for. I'm always intrigued, and often amused, at the circular nature of this work: we struggle through intense and complex issues only to wind up where we began, just hopefully a little wiser and more skilled. On any given day, our problem focusing, dealing with our emotions, or making a decision might best be solved by taking a nap or a walk, or eating a decent lunch. We will benefit no one, least of all ourselves, if we aren't taking adequate care of our physical health.

Adequate Sleep

I won't go into much depth on these topics, since there is so much information available on them. However, it's worth quickly summarizing some basic points. First, pay attention to both the quantity and the quality of your sleep. How much sleep do you typically need, and how much do you regularly get? Adjust your routines or expectations to close that gap. Also, take steps to increase your ability to get a good night's sleep: practice relaxation, meditation, and exercise every day. Don't check your email for at least an hour before going to sleep. If you suffer from persistent anxiety that keeps you from sleeping well, seek help and advice. Sleep is such a fundamental human need, and yet it is surprisingly easy to overlook or ignore.

Healthy Eating

Eating well is easy (and not so easy). We already make time to eat every day, so simply pay attention to what you put in your body. Scrutinize your current choices; for one week, conduct a personal audit of only what you eat. Now, how can you improve your eating habits? Michael Pollan, in his book *In Defense of Food*, says healthy eating can be summarized in seven words: *Eat food. Not too much. Mostly plants.* I agree, but I think it really comes down to one word: *awareness.* Then, successfully changing habits, and maintaining them, really depends on three words: *Love your food.* Enjoy eating. Enjoy cooking or choosing food that is right for you. Keep track of what you actually eat. Count calories. Try it. It works.

Plenty of Exercise

Even if we sleep well and eat well, a too-sedentary life can undermine our physical health (and lead to disease). Again, simply paying attention to your body is the most essential step. To take care of this body, do a little exercise every day, and do lots some days. Create a plan. Work your plan. Seek company to create mutual support. Be good to your body.

Your Most Important Relationship: YOU

Ultimately, all the tools and practices presented in this book are ways to benefit yourself and to benefit others. Whether focused outward or inward, they generate a virtuous circle of care, intention, and effectiveness that benefits all of us. In chapter 5, we discussed our communication with others through confident speech, curious questioning, and compassionate listening. We need to bring those same skills to bear, and take the same care, in our own inner life. People are all essentially the same: we are simple and straightforward, just seeking happiness, just wanting others to be happy. We are also quite complex and multifaceted. We contain a variety of aspirations and wishes, fears and doubts. These express themselves in a multitude of voices; sometimes they are aligned, sometimes competing. An effective way to take care of and benefit ourselves is to become more familiar with these voices. Pay close attention to the ways in which you speak to yourself. Do you speak confidently and listen compassionately? Are you curious about your inner life? We are almost always holding an inner conversation with ourselves that is influencing and directing our emotions and actions. The more we can become familiar with these voices, the more effective we can be.

Here is an exercise for exploring and understanding your voices.

Exploring Your Voices

Let's start with a short guided visualization. However you are sitting, change your position, even slightly. This is a way of bringing your attention to your body. Notice how you are sitting. See if you can relax; relax your shoulders, back, face, and jaw. At the same time notice your energy. See if you can sit while being both relaxed and alert at the same time. This is my aim and intention for accomplishing most things: to be relaxed and alert.

Now, bring your attention to your breathing. Notice that you are breathing. See if you can breathe all the way in and all the way out. Whatever thoughts and concerns may arise in your mind, notice these and gently bring your attention back to your breath.

Now, let's explore some of your internal voices.

Let's begin with the voice of appreciation. Let thoughts arise about a person or something that your appreciate, a loved one, a friend, or a place that is meaningful to you. Picture this person or object and notice what appreciation feels like. Where in your body do you feel appreciation; is it in your chest or stomach, or maybe not any clear place? What does your voice of appreciation sound like and feel like within you? Stay here for a few moments.

Now, let go of that voice, of all voices, and bring your attention back to your breath and back to your body.

Now, let's explore your voice of fear. Think for a moment about a situation that brings up fear. If several situations come up, notice what these situations have in common. What do you worry about? What fears do you harbor for yourself or your family? What fears do you have about your work or for the world? Let your voice of fear arise. If you usually suppress this voice, allow it; we are just exploring. Listen to this voice with open curiosity. Where in your body is the voice of fear? What does this voice sound like and feel like? Stay with this voice for a few minutes.

Now, let go of that voice, of all voices, and bring your attention back to your breath and back to your body.

Now, let's explore your voice of hope. What are you hoping for, from this exercise or book, from your day today? What do you hope for yourself and your family? What hopes do you have for your work and for the world? Let your voice of hope arise. If you usually suppress this voice, allow it; we are just exploring. Listen to this voice with open curiosity. Where in your body is the voice of hope? What does this voice sound like? Stay with this voice for a few minutes.

Now, let go of that voice, of all voices, and bring your attention back to your breath and back to your body.

Lastly, let's explore your voice of wisdom — whatever that might mean for you. Think of a person you consider wise, compassionate, or generous. Think of something you said or did or accomplished that you felt really good about; think of a decision you made that had a positive outcome. Maybe wisdom is a spiritual voice of just appreciating being alive, beyond good or bad, right or wrong. Allow this voice; we are just exploring. Listen to this voice with open curiosity. Where in your body do you experience wisdom? What does this voice sound like and feel like? If this is easy, great! If this is not so easy, and if not much is happening, also great! Just remain relaxed and alert, exploring.

Now, let go of that voice, of all voices, and bring your attention back to your breath and back to your body. Sit quietly for a few minutes, following the breath, being aware.

Now, open your eyes. Let your consciousness return to the room.

When you finish, take a few minutes to reflect on what happened. How was that for you? Was hearing these voices of appreciation, fear, hope, and wisdom easy or difficult? Was your thinking mind calm or agitated? Did you notice other voices arise — judgments and self-criticism, or voices of kindness and generosity? Try this exercise again and explore other voices, such as jealousy, joy, worry, or patience. You could also do this as a written exercise, or artistic expression, letting your voices come forth on the page.

Good Friends Are Your Prosperity

A study followed the lives of 268 Harvard students from the classes of 1942, '43, and '44 for more than 70 years. When asked what he learned from the study, Dr. George Vaillant, the psychiatrist who conducted the study for more than 42 years, responded, "The only thing that really matters in life [is] your relationships with other people."

— "What Makes Us Happy?," Atlantic magazine, June 2009

What a powerful conclusion to a seventy-year study: "The only thing that really matters in life [is] your relationships with other people." I think we all know this, and yet it is easy to forget in the midst of the pace and challenges of daily life.

What are your life goals as you've defined them while reading this book? How do you define prosperity? Almost by default, we often think of prosperity in terms of money, financial security, or standard of living. We think of our life goals in terms of significant achievements: founding a company, writing a book, changing the world, leaving a legacy. Accordingly, we can fall into the habit of evaluating the people we meet by how well they can help us, as necessary means to our ends, but our true prosperity *is* our relationships. This is another way we can change the way we conduct the business of our lives — by valuing the people in them, not what they can do to help us.

When it comes to issues of prosperity, it is also easy to feel a sense of scarcity, that we never have enough time or money. But when we look closely, the most poignant feelings of scarcity come from a lack of connection. No amount of money or time soothes a loss of community, if our lives become bereft of close emotional connections with other people. Abundance, safety, and happiness come from the richness of our relationships with family members, friends, coworkers, and others.

However, at least in much of the United States and the developed world, feeling separate and isolated seems to be the accepted state for many people. We live in separate units, drive alone in cars, and avoid eye contact in public places. Developing friendships often involves intention and effort. Of course, seeking connection can involve the risk of rejection. Social media have increased our reach, but often in a shallow way. Online "social media friends" are not necessarily real friends unless or until they cross the digital threshold: spending time with us, having conversations, sharing experiences and hopes, caring.

So, to increase your prosperity, explore ways to develop the quality and richness of your existing relationships. Identify people whom you want to develop a deeper connection or friendship with, and schedule time with them. Ask colleagues to join you for walks or for lunch. While cultivating existing relationships, explore ways you might cultivate new ones as well.

Have Real Conversations

It is easy to go an entire day, or many days, without having a real conversation with another person. What is a real conversation? It is one that includes your emotions; it's a discussion about something you care about in which you express that caring. It can be anything that matters: personal issues, work issues, your gardening, your hopes and dreams. In some way, you show up in the presence of another; you are open, unguarded, even vulnerable. It doesn't have to be confessional; it can be providing the space for someone else to be open and vulnerable. Your part of the conversation may be to listen.

This is as essential for our well-being and health as eating and sleeping, which is why I include it in the personal audit I describe in chapter 4. If you're unsure how many real conversations you have each day, keep track and become aware.

Join Small Groups

In the book *The Social Animal, New York Times* writer David Brooks cites a research statistic that "being part of a small group that meets monthly brings more personal happiness than having your salary doubled." That's another very interesting standard for evaluating the prosperity in your life. How many small groups are you part of? Any? If you are not part of a group, consider joining one or creating one, of any kind — a book group or discussion group, a yoga class or cycling club, a volunteer or community group. Be part of something either connected to or distinct from your work and home life. It's hard to feel alone when others rely on us, turn to us, need us — when we are part of joint efforts and shared purpose.

As this implies, creating a satisfying sense of community takes work and commitment. Many of us are already part of multiple groups or communities that we barely notice and don't take the time or effort to cultivate. These communities include our neighbors, people supporting our chosen profession or our favorite hobbies, and the larger communities of the town or city where we live. I once helped create a community of executive coaches, a group of eight that met about every six weeks for many years. I'm also part of an Old Zen Men group that meets for a long weekend once a year. We have known each other for more than thirty years. I have been surprised at how important this group has become for me, even though it meets infrequently. Another important community for me is my friends from the socially responsible business world. I've been a member of a nonprofit organization called Social Venture Network (SVN) for many years, and I attend SVN conferences twice a year. These are work events, in which I'm focused on business, but unexpectedly, it has become an important and nurturing community of friends. As it turns out, sometimes blurring these distinctions is part of what being a socially responsible businessperson is all about.

Me Inc. — Your Personal Brand

Personal branding is a hot topic these days. To a degree, it all began with the article "The Brand Called You" by Tom Peters in 1997. Peters wrote:

Regardless of age, regardless of position, regardless of the business we happen to be in, all of us need to understand the importance of branding. We are CEOs of our own companies: Me Inc. To be in business today, our most important job is to be head marketer for the brand called You.

If, within this chapter's paradox, one essential aspect of balance is to approach business in more emotional, personal terms, then the other and opposite aspect is to see ourselves in more businesslike terms. What is our persona, our story, our offering, our brand? I agree with Peters: we ignore our brand at our own peril. Our brand is how we represent the business of our self. Our brand is how we are (or would like to be) perceived by others. This determines whether others believe that we meet their needs, whether we offer useful solutions or help, whether we are trustworthy and reliable. As all businesses today know, it is vital to pay attention to and care for your brand.

We all have a brand, whether we want one or not, whether we consciously construct one or have one given to us. Buddha had a brand, as do the Dalai Lama and President Obama, and even those claiming not to have a brand — no brand is also a brand. Our brand is part of our story. What story do you tell of yourself when you meet someone new? When used with integrity, our brand expresses who we are and what we stand for; it encapsulates the way we see the world and its problems, and the nature of the solutions we offer. Our brand expresses our values.

Like anything, a brand can be misused. The word itself has negative connotations. A brand can be the ultimate corporate fraud or scam when it's used to peddle the perception of value without actually providing value. But isn't this a struggle we all face? We express noble values or intentions even while knowing that there is a gap between these and our actions. Further, we cannot control how others perceive us. Our brand's reputation will differ from one person to the next. In the West, many people regard the Dalai Lama as a model of wisdom and humility. The Chinese government has a different perception.

Despite this lack of control over perception, we still must tend to our public self or persona. To benefit others, to benefit ourselves, we explore what we offer, and so we arrive back at our first paradox: Know yourself, forget yourself, write your story. Your effort to create a solid, clearly identifiable self and a solid unchanging brand is both a worthy, even necessary, effort and also essentially impossible. It is not wholly real, complete, or lasting: you will change, others will change, markets change, needs change — your brand will change.

So keep walking, keep balancing, keep embracing paradox:

- Articulate your values and evaluate your life to ensure your actions are aligned with them.
- Communicate your brand, your authentic offering, the best you can. Then ask for and listen to feedback, and change in response to it. Be flexible and persistent.
- Notice and be honest about your strengths and your limitations, and work to close the gaps between your brand, your perception of yourself, and the perceptions of others.

At the same time, remember that you are not a brand. You are not a story. You simply are. Even as you tend to your brand, practice the art of "being nobody." This is a terrific, freeing practice. It means letting go of trying to be anyone special, of trying to be in control, of trying to fix or hold on to or gain or offer anything, especially yourself. Let yourself just be, a happy, compassionate nobody, a paradox. Yes, know yourself, forget yourself!

Step from the Top of a Hundred-Foot Pole

Here is a simple and penetrating story from the Zen tradition about taking care of the world and taking care of yourself. It goes like this:

> You who sit on the top of a hundred-foot pole,
> Although you have entered the Way, it is not genuine.
> Take a step from the top of the pole
> And the entire universe is no different than you.

This is the Zen version of the tightrope walker and the Zen response to the paradox of how we both benefit others and benefit ourselves. If you think you and the world are different, your understanding is not developed enough; it is not wide enough, not genuine. Make just a little more effort by letting go of whatever gets in your way of seeing that you are the world and the world is you.

Stepping from a hundred-foot pole is to step out from behind yourself and the habits that hold you back. This doesn't mean to avoid or ignore your pain and confusion, and your messy, sometimes challenging, sometimes seemingly impossible life circumstances. Instead, stepping from the hundred-foot pole is just the opposite — you step directly into your feelings and emotions, your motivations and conditions. You step into and embrace whatever is most messy and difficult, as well as joyful and wise. Look deeply, gently, openly.

It seems at times as though we have no choice but to act as though the world is permanent, solid, and predictable, and at the

same time, we must realize that everything around us is impermanent, fluid, and unpredictable. If we go too far toward believing in
permanence, we will be thrown when something unexpected happens. If we lean too far toward a belief in impermanence, we may
fall into the trap of not setting clear goals, not achieving what is
within our potential, and living irresponsibly. This can be a way
of trying to protect ourselves from failure or sometimes of trying
to protect ourselves from success. The secret of successful business practice and of life practice is finding the balance between
control and letting go; it's understanding that, though little is
within our control, we must act with complete responsibility.

In one of his talks, Shunryu Suzuki commented on this story,
saying, "The secret is just to say 'Yes!' and jump off from here.
Then there is no problem. It means to be yourself in the present
moment, always yourself, without sticking to an old self. You forget yourself and are refreshed."

This short, pithy four-line story points to the dilemma that
we all have, that we all face, all experience. How do we balance all
of these seemingly impossible demands and priorities? How can I
be happy, feel safe, be satisfied, provide for myself and family, and
help others? What is this life? What does it mean to be an authentic human being in the realm of family, work, smart phones, relationships, love, hate, birth, and death? We are all perched on the
top of a hundred-foot pole. Together. It is a very wide pole. So
wide, there is no place to fall.

Just say yes.

Epilogue

LIVE LONG AND PROSPER!

I love how the process of writing is itself a dance of knowing myself and forgetting myself, recalling and weaving stories and emotions while getting out of my own way as I search for the right words, the perfect words, and simultaneously let go or at least reduce my own judgments. Much like the practice of mindfulness and meditation, just being present, right here, right now — opening, searching, sometimes holding on, sometimes letting go. Words, ideas, and stories bubbling up from some mysterious well within. When I'm lucky, the words seem to choose me.

Today, as I walked along a trail in the Tennessee Valley, a beautiful path on the California coast leading to the Pacific Ocean, I felt a deep sadness and longing, for no apparent reason. "This place is so beautiful," I said to myself, and I knew that it would never look this way again — vibrant wildflowers, puffy white clouds, fog in the distance, the chill and heat of a spring afternoon. And I wondered, How many more visits during this lifetime, if any, will I make to this special valley?

I'm struck that as I'm completing this book, the scenery of my life is changing. My first book, *Z.B.A. Zen of Business Administration*, was written from the vantage point of being CEO of Brush

Dance publishing company. Just as I was completing that book, I was leaving Brush Dance and transitioning into a new business: that of an executive coach and leadership consultant, helping to guide other business leaders. Now, as I put the final touches on this book, I find myself transitioning again: leaving my consultancy practice to become a CEO. Yet while my role is changing, my focus is the same. As CEO of SIYLI, the Search Inside Yourself Leadership Institute, I will expand the model I helped to develop for trainings within Google, integrating mindfulness and emotional intelligence and neuroscience. SIYLI's vision is to aid and inspire enlightened leaders worldwide; its mission is to help create the conditions for world peace.

I'm pleased that I now have a manual — this book! — to help me find my way as a CEO, and as a husband, father, and human being. I sometimes notice as a coach and consultant that, even as I'm speaking with my clients, a voice in my head is saying, "You should be paying attention, Lesser. There is much you could be learning from these words that are coming out of this mouth, *your* mouth."

I'm reminded of a famous Zen story (sorry, I just can't help myself) from ninth-century China about a Zen teacher who could sometimes be heard having a stern conversation with himself:

"Master Zuigan!" he would call out.
"Yes?" he would reply.
"Are you here?"
"Yes!" he would respond to himself.

How sweet, how odd, how wonderful! This Zen story underscores how challenging it can be to be present, to show up, to be free and flexible for our lives. And Zuigan didn't have a smart phone, the Internet, or television to contend with. It seems that showing up and being fully present, fully alive, has always been challenging.

I like Zuigan's practice, and I recommend it as the last practice in this book. Ask yourself at any time, at any moment: "Am I here?" And then without hesitating answer, "Yes!" We can all try this when listening to another person, driving a car, eating our breakfast: Are you here? Check in with yourself — what's happening, right now, with your thinking, your feelings? What's in your heart?

I leave you, dear reader, with wishes for peace and happiness. And as we often say at the end of the Search Inside Yourself programs at Google, "Live long and prosper."

ACKNOWLEDGMENTS

I'm often asked, "What is your process for writing? With all of your activities, how do you find the time? What is your writing discipline?" I must admit to having neither the time to write nor a writing discipline. For me, there are several essential ingredients for creating the conditions for a book to emerge: 1.) a publisher who believes in me ("So, when are you going to write another book?"; and the dreaded, "Here is your manuscript deadline."); 2.) a collaborator in the form of a talented editor; 3.) spiritual teachers and friends; 4.) colleagues and community; and 5.) a supportive family.

1. Publisher: Thank you, New World Library — especially Jason Gardner, Marc Allen, Monique Muhlenkamp, and Munro Magruder — for your support and encouragement. And to Stephanie Tade, my agent.
2. Collaborator: My appreciation to Jeff Campbell, editor extraordinaire. Jeff helped shape this book in its early stages, and he helped birth it at every stage. And to Jennifer Futernick, for inserting a little extra poetry and love, just when it needed it.

3. Spiritual teachers and friends: Thank you to my core
   spiritual teachers and several dharma supporters: Michael
   Wenger and Norman Fischer; Vickie Austin, Chris Fortin,
   Bruce Fortin, Steve Weintraub, Steve Stucky, Peter van
   der Sterre, Rick Levine, Ken Sawyer, Marc Alexander,
   Meg Alexander, ARobin Orden, and Steve Gross.

4. Community: Many thanks to my amazing partners at
   Google's Search Inside Yourself (SIY) program (and
   now SIYLI), Chade-Meng Tan, Philippe Goldin, Mirabai
   Bush, and Yvonne Ginsberg, and all the Googlers who
   have attended and helped shape the SIY program.

   Thanks to Peter Strugatz, Katie Wood, Roger Housden, and Barbara Disco for reading chapters, and for
   the encouragement from my core Wednesday night sitting group who listened to me read many drafts: David
   Maxwell, Dharna Obermeir, Nadine Gay, David Stoebel,
   and Florian Brody. And to the memory of my dear friend
   Carole Harris.

   Here, I also must name a few of many from the
   Social Venture Network community: Deborah Nelson,
   Erin Roach, Aaron Lamstein, David Leventhal, Elliot
   Hoffman, Jay Harris, and Judi Cohen.

   Also, I owe a debt to a few of my many coaching and
   leadership friends — Jackie McGrath, Simon Turkalj,
   Ken Schatz, Lucinda Rhys, and Linda Curtis — and to
   my coaching clients.

5. Family: With gratitude to my son, Jason, and daughter,
   Carol, for their light and love, and to my wife, Lee, not
   only for reading every word of the manuscript but most
   of all for helping me to know myself and forget myself.

NOTES

Chapter 1: From Paradox to Insight

Page 14, *"That image reminds me of a story," I told him. "It's an old Zen story"*: Adapted from Thomas Cleary, trans., "Case 25, Yanguan's 'Rhinoceros Fan,'" in *Book of Serenity: One Hundred Zen Dialogues* (Boston: Shambhala, 1988).

Chapter 2: Effectiveness: The Backward Step

Page 34, *There is a Zen story from the seventh century in China, part of a collection*: Adapted from Thomas Cleary and J. C. Cleary, trans., "Case 14, Yun Men's Appropriate Statement," in *The Blue Cliff Record* (Boston: Shambhala, 1977).

Chapter 3: More Clear Than Clear

Page 45, *There is a famous thirteenth-century story about Dogen, the founder of Zen*: Adapted from Thomas Cleary, trans., *Timeless Spring: A Soto Zen Anthology* (Helena, WA: Wheelwright Publishing, 1980).

Page 49, *This is completely aligned with a 2009 study showing that optimal performance*: Y. Tang and M. Posner, "Attention Training and Attention State Training," *Trends in Cognitive Sciences* (May 2009).

Page 55, *There is another famous Zen dialogue from ancient China about a monk and a teacher*: Adapted from Robert Aitken, trans., "Case 7, Chao-chou:

'Wash Your Bowl,' " in *The Gateless Barrier: The Wu-Men Kuan* (New York: North Point Press, 1991).

Chapter 4: Know Yourself, Forget Yourself

Page 69, *One of the most famous dialogues from the Zen tradition is between Bodhidharma*: Adapted from Thomas Cleary and J. C. Cleary, trans., "Case 1, The Highest Meaning of the Holy Truths," in *The Blue Cliff Record* (Boston: Shambhala, 1977).

Page 77, *One study, done with workers in technology companies, demonstrated that practicing attention training*: Richard Davidson et al., "Alterations in Brain and Immune Function Produced by Mindfulness Meditation," *Psychosomatic Medicine* 65 (2003): 564–70.

Page 78, *Recent studies have shown that writing regularly leads to greater self-understanding*: For more on this, see Martin Seligman, *Learned Optimism: How to Change Your Mind and Your Life* (New York: Vintage/Random House, 2006); and S. P. Spera, E. D. Buhrfeind, and J. W. Pennebaker, "Expressive Writing and Coping with Job Loss," *Academy of Management Journal* (1994).

Chapter 5: Be Confident, Question Everything

Page 109, *Abraham Maslow described the abiding potential of human beings by coining the term*: Abraham Maslow, *Toward a Psychology of Being* (New York: Van Nostrand Reinhold, 1968).

Page 109, *Peter Senge, in* The Fifth Discipline, *describes confidence*: Peter Senge, *The Fifth Discipline* (New York: Crown Business, 2006).

Page 111, *In an interview with Charlie Rose, Ray Dalio — CEO of Bridgewater*: Ray Dalio, interview by Charlie Rose, *Charlie Rose Show*, October 20, 2011, www.youtube.com/watch?v=Ve2_5F_e8IY.

Page 111, *Daniel Goleman, in his writings on emotional intelligence, describes confidence*: Daniel Goleman, *Working with Emotional Intelligence* (New York: Bantam, 2000).

Page 118, *There is a seventh-century Zen story I like to tell to illustrate this*: Adapted from Thomas Cleary and J. C. Cleary, trans., "Case 55, Tao Wu's Condolence Call," in *The Blue Cliff Record* (Boston: Shambhala, 1977).

Page 120, *In a 2011* New York Times *story, Daniel Kahneman describes how wanting our ideas*: Daniel Kahneman, "Don't Blink! The Hazards of Confidence," *New York Times*, October 19, 2011.

Page 124, *"Walking" by Nagarjuna, as translated by Stephen Batchelor in* Verses from the Center: Stephen Batchelor, *Verses from the Center* (New York: Riverhead, 2000).

Page 126, *In this ancient Zen story, one teacher is walking along the road and comes across*: Adapted from Thomas Cleary, trans., "Case 20, Dizang's 'Nearness,'" in *Book of Serenity: One Hundred Zen Dialogues* (Boston: Shambhala, 1988).

Chapter 6: Fight for Change, Accept What Is

Page 150, *I'm reminded of a few lines of poetry from David Whyte*: David Whyte, "Sweet Darkness," in *The House of Belonging* (Langley, WA: Many Rivers Press, 2002).

Page 167, *One story in particular is quite succinct, and famous, and speaks directly*: Adapted from Thomas Cleary and J. C. Cleary, trans., "Case 2, 'The Ultimate Path Is without Difficulty,'" in *The Blue Cliff Record* (Boston: Shambhala, 1977).

Chapter 7: Embrace Emotion, Embody Equanimity

Page 180, *The most famous example in today's organizational effectiveness lore is the story of General Motors*: For more on GM's story, see "NUMMI," *This American Life*, National Public Radio, March 26, 2010, www .thisamericanlife.org/radio-archives/episode/403/nummi.

Page 183, *Numerous studies have demonstrated that working skillfully with emotions leads to greater productivity*: Details from these studies came from a lecture by Daniel Goleman, "Social Intelligence: The New Science of Human Relationship," Authors@Google, Mountain View, CA, August 3, 2007.

Page 185, *David Rock, in his book* Your Brain at Work, *beautifully describes and unpacks this dynamic*: David Rock, *Your Brain at Work* (New York: HarperBusiness, 2009).

Page 189, *A very earnest Zen student asks his teacher, "How can I avoid the discomfort"*: Adapted from Thomas Cleary and J. C. Cleary, trans., "Case 43, Tung Shan's No Cold or Heat," in *The Blue Cliff Record* (Boston: Shambhala, 1977).

Page 194, *In the book* The Art of Happiness at Work *by the Dalai Lama and Howard Cutler*: His Holiness the Dalai Lama and Howard Cutler, *The Art of Happiness at Work* (New York: Riverhead Trade, 2004).

Chapter 8: Benefit Others, Benefit Yourself

Page 219, *There is a famous story from the Zen tradition about two teachers meeting on the road*: Adapted from Thomas Cleary, trans., "Case 12, Dizang Planting the Fields," in *Book of Serenity, One Hundred Zen Dialogues* (Boston: Shambhala, 1988).

Page 234, *In the bestselling book* Blessed Unrest: How the Largest Social Movement in History Is Restoring Grace, Social Justice, and Beauty to the World, *Paul Hawken*: Paul Hawken, *Blessed Unrest: How the Largest Social Movement in History Is Restoring Grace, Social Justice, and Beauty to the World* (New York: Penguin, 2008).

Page 245, *Michael Pollan, in his book* In Defense of Food, *says healthy eating*: Michael Pollan, *In Defense of Food: An Eater's Manifesto* (New York: Penguin, 2008).

Page 248, *A study followed the lives of 268 Harvard students from the classes*: Joshua Wolf Shenk, "What Makes Us Happy?" *The Atlantic* (June 2009).

Page 250, *In the book* The Social Animal, New York Times *writer David Brooks cites a research*: David Brooks, *The Social Animal: The Hidden Sources of Love, Character, and Achievement* (New York: Random House, 2011).

Page 251, *To a degree, it all began with the article* "The Brand Called You" *by Tom Peters in 1997*: Tom Peters, "The Brand Called You," *Fast Company* (August 31, 1997), www.fastcompany.com/magazine/10/brandyou.html.

Page 254, *Here is a simple and penetrating story from the Zen tradition about taking care of the world*: Adapted from Robert Aitken, trans., "Case 46, Shih-shuang: 'Step from the Top of the Pole,'" in *The Gateless Barrier: The Wu-Men Kuan* (New York: North Point Press, 1991).

Epilogue: Live Long and Prosper!

Page 258, *I'm reminded of a famous Zen story (sorry, I just can't help myself) from ninth-century China*: Adapted from Robert Aitken, trans., "Case 12, Jui-yen Calls 'Master,'" in *The Gateless Barrier: The Wu-Men Kuan* (New York: North Point Press, 1991).

RECOMMENDED READING

So many books. Here are just a few that I find myself often recommending.

Chödrön, Pema. *Taking the Leap*. Boston: Shambhala, 2009.

Collins, Jim. *Good to Great: Why Some Companies Make the Leap...and Others Don't*. New York: HarperBusiness, 2001.

Goleman, Daniel. *Destructive Emotions: How Can We Overcome Them? A Scientific Dialogue with the Dalai Lama*. New York: Bantam Books, 2003.

Hanh, Thich Nhat. *Breathe, You Are Alive!: The Sutra on the Full Awareness of Breathing*. Berkeley, CA: Parallax Press, 1996.

Housden, Roger, ed. *Risking Everything: 110 Poems of Love and Revelation*. New York: Harmony Books, 2003.

Lusseyran, Jacques. *And There Was Light: Autobiography of Jacques Lusseyran, Blind Hero of the French Resistance*. Sandpoint, ID: Morning Light Press, 2006.

Okumura, Shohaku. *Realizing Genjokoan*. Somerville, MA: Wisdom Publications, 2010.

Oliver, Mary. *New and Selected Poems*, Vol. 1. Boston: Beacon Press, 2005.

Stone, Douglas, Bruce Patton, and Sheila Heen. *Difficult Conversations: How to Discuss What Matters Most*. New York: Penguin, 1999.

Suzuki, Shunryu. *Not Always So*. New York: HarperCollins, 2002.

Tan, Chade-Meng. *Search Inside Yourself*. New York: HarperOne, 2012.

Whyte, David. *The House of Belonging*. Langley, WA: Many Rivers Press, 2002.

INDEX

B

backward step, 35–36
Baker, Richard, 24
balance
> benefitting others/oneself, 252
> defined, 144, 242
> effectiveness and, 32–33, 49
> emotions/equanimity, 178
> lives out of, 13–15
> paradox and, 17–18

balance sheets, 158
Bateson, Gregory, 18
being, joy of, 179, 204–5
"being nobody," practice of, 253–54
benchmarks, 165
Benefit Corporations, 240–41
benefitting oneself
> Action Plan, 217–18
> balance and, 242, 252
> benefits of, 7
> branding, personal, 251–54
> health, 243–45
> inner life, 245–48
> paradox and, 5–6, 252–55

benefitting others
> Action Plan, 217–18
> alignment, 226–34
> balance and, 242, 252
> benefits of, 7
> business practice improvements, 234–41
> impact, 223–25
> paradox and, 5–6, 252–55
> spheres of influence, 219–23

blame, 184, 188–89, 201–2, 232
Blessed Unrest (Hawken), 234–35
blind spots, 79–81
"board-carrying fellow" (Zen expression), 17–18
Bodhidharma (wandering Buddhist monk), 69–71, 79
body
> emotions in, 202–3
> focusing attention on, 75–76

body language, 116
"Brand Called You, The" (Peters), 251–52
branding, personal, 218, 251–54

breathing, 31–33, 75–76, 158, 203, 246
brokenness, 209–10
Brooks, David, 250
Brown, Ed, 213
Brush Dance (publishing company),
> author as CEO of, 25–26, 99, 105, 129–32, 176, 186–87, 215–17, 219–20, 257–58
> business failures of, 186–87
> business strategy of, 129–32
> founding of, 25, 129
> greeting cards published by, 34, 91
> growth of, 25–26
> impact of, 223–24
> vision of, 215–17

Buber, Martin, 45
bucket lists, 168
Buddha
> on acceptance, 168–69
> as effectiveness teacher, 47–50
> spiritual practice of, 82–83

Buddhism
> change in, 120
> Eightfold Path, 48, 95
> equanimity in, 196
> Five Hindrances, 52–55
> Four Noble Truths, 47–49
> Four Seals, 50–52
> as middle way, 8, 49
> *See also* Zen Buddhism

budgets, 158–60
business
> assembly-line model of, 180–82
> change in practices, 234–41
> emotional well-being in, 179–84
> Zen Buddhism and, 28–29

business leadership
> acceptance vs. change in, 141–42
> confidence and questioning in, 110–11
> confidence in, 112–20
> emotional competencies in, 183
> not knowing in, 129–32
> presence and listening in, 116–18
> trust and speech in, 113–15
> vision and inspiration in, 118–19

business plans, 142, 143, 162–65, 218, 228–29

"Walking with Confidence" (exercise),
125–26
Way-seeking mind, 143–46, 153, 154
Weintraub, Steve, 130
Weiss, Pamela, 34
well-being, 74
Whyte, David, 150
wisdom, voice of, 247–48
work
    decision making regarding, 37–41
    happiness index for, 166
    "meaningful," 220
    personal audit for, 161
workplace
    climate of, 218, 232–34
    dehumanizing, equanimity in, 194–95
    healthy, 237–39
world, the, 219–23
Wu (Chinese emperor), 69–71

Y

Your Brain at Work (Rock), 185

Z

ZBA Associates, 26, 229–30
Z.B.A. Zen of Business Administration
    (Lesser), 257–58

Zen Buddhism
    business and, 28–29
    emergence of, 49, 70
    paradoxical approach of, 49–50
    precepts of, 23, 94–95, 241
    problem solving in, 46–47, 145
Zen expressions, 17–18
Zen stories, 45–46
    appropriate responses, 34
    hot and cold, 189–90
    how to use, 55–56, 77–78, 119, 126–27
    "I won't say," 118–19
    "not knowing is most intimate," 126–28
    one-hundred-foot pole, 254–55
    paradox in, 18
    purpose of, 55, 57
    rhinoceros-horn fan, 14–15
    self-knowledge, 69–72
    "wash your bowl," 55–57
    "the world," 219
Zuigan, Master, 258–59